HOW TO HEAR
GOD'S VOICE:
Intro to Dream Interpretation

BY
DEBORAH SANDOW

ISBN 978-1-60920-127-2
Printed in the United States of America

© 2017 Debbi Sandow
All rights reserved

Library of Congress-in-Publication Data

API
Ajoyin Publishing, Inc.
P.O. Box 342
Three Rivers, MI 49093
www.ajoyin.com

Please direct your inquiries to admin@ajoyin.com

TABLE OF CONTENTS

PREFACE

BETWEEN 2010 AND 2014, I had four miscarriages. I was perplexed. What was God doing? In our first seven years of marriage, Patrick and I had exhausted our finances and our emotions trying every means to have a baby, to no avail. Now I was forty-five with four adopted children, the youngest in middle school, and I was pregnant. What?

Painfully and confused, I miscarried. I became pregnant a second time; same result, a miscarriage. A third pregnancy, a fourth: miscarriage, miscarriage. Was this some evil trick? What was God doing? I was so angry at God.

Thank God for Christian television! One morning as I lay in bed, struggling emotionally, spiritually, and physically, I watched television. A preacher said, "It is an evil man that attacks another man. It is a most evil man that attacks another man's child to get to the man." I realized at that moment God did not cause the miscarriages; the enemy, Satan, had. I cried out in repentance. I was blaming a God that had proven Himself good and faithful so many times. I began to ask God to take this pain and use it for His glory. That's when God dropped into my heart four Bible studies. I became pregnant again, this time with Bible studies. I wrote these Bible studies out of the pain, with joy returning. *Study of Prayer, Why Do Bad Things Happen, How to Hear God's Voice: Intro to Prophecy,* and *How to Hear God's Voice: Intro to Dream Interpretation* were birthed.

By no means are these Bible studies the complete authority on these subjects. Nonetheless, I pray that these Bible studies whet your appetite for more. I have filled these Bible studies with many scriptures so that you will have a good foundation on which to build your knowledge of and your relationship with God. I have also added a recommended reading list at the end. I have learned so many things from these great men and women of God. I pray that these studies will help you desire more of God and that you have fun on this journey as you study the scriptures.

Acknowledgment

I CAN NEVER FULLY EXPRESS MY gratitude to my King Jesus. He has given me so much. He has saved me. He has sanctified me. He has given me purpose. He has given me the desires of my heart, even when I didn't know what they were.

I am grateful for the wonderful parents He gave me. Ed and Jan Billingsley have been loving and supportive parents to me. I am so thankful to them for all they have done for me. They have made sacrifices for me and have given of themselves to me. It would take volumes to write all they have done for me.

I am grateful for the amazing husband God has given me. I made a list in middle school of what I wanted in a husband. Patrick James Sandow has exceeded that list many times over. He has laughed at my weirdness. He has wiped my tears. He has made me laugh when I most needed it. He has held me up when the frustrations and hurts of this world have tried to knock me down. He has been patient with me as I was learning about my spiritual gift. He has helped bring me to my senses; common sense is not my gift. He has been the constant that I needed in this inconsistent world. He has been exactly what I needed when I needed it. Only God could have known how much I needed a man like Patrick. Thank you, Patrick, for your abundant love and for coming with me on this crazy ride.

I am blessed by God with four amazing children: Spencer, Emmanuel, Deborah Joy, and Aubrey. I am grateful for all the lessons my children have taught me. Thank you, guys, for putting up with my terrible housekeeping and subpar cooking. Thank you for having patience with me as I preached and tried to teach you what I was learning. You are all a treasure to me.

I am grateful for so many wonderful friends and family members that have prayed with and for me. You are such an important part of my growth in the Lord. You have taught me what it means to be a "Body of Christ."

I would like to acknowledge three special ladies, Martha, Cynthia, and Jo. These wonderful ladies met with me weekly. They allowed me to try this material out with them as the students. Their insights, suggestions, and accountability greatly helped me finish this project. I am eternally grateful for their love and support.

All Scripture quotations, unless otherwise indicated, are taken from *New King James Version* (NKJV).

How To Hear God's Voice: Intro to Dream Interpretation week one

DOES GOD SPEAK THROUGH DREAMS? Absolutely! Here's what happened to me: I was never a dreamer. When I had a dream I would wake up and scratch my head, or I would wonder, "What did I eat before I went to bed last night?" My husband, on the other hand, was an avid dreamer. In fact, he went through a period where he was dreaming so much that it really bothered him. It got so bad that he tried forcing himself to stay awake so that he would not dream.

Around that time, a friend stopped by. She had just heard of a Bible class and wondered if I would be interested in taking it with her. It was on dream interpretation. She had my attention.

When I asked my husband about it, he said a resounding "yes".

Off to New Hampshire I went for a week-long course by John Paul Jackson called "The Art of Hearing God 101." Three months later I took another class, "Dreams and Visions 202," and six months later, "Dream Workshop 202." These classes took the lid off my little box. I thought God had limited ways of communicating. I was terribly wrong.

After the classes, God gave my husband and me some clarification on what God was saying in the dreams. Ever since, both of our dream lives have been encouraging and comforting and informative. I believe as you go through this study, it will be the same for you. No, it's not just the pizza you ate last night!

I know that there are many fears and thoughts about dreams. So I want to take a moment and ask:

Why are you doing this study?

_____

_____

What questions do you have about dreams?

_____

_____

I ask these questions to help you focus on why you want to do this study. Is it because you want to hear God in a new way? Do you have friends that have dreams and don't know what the dreams mean? Do you have a disturbing dream from your childhood that you still remember? It is my prayer that as you go through this study, you will have those questions answered, and your fears quieted.

Some questions might be: Is dream interpretation a biblical topic? Yes! Are there dreams in the Bible? A resounding yes! Are dreams interpreted? Yes!

Let's take a look at two well-known dreamers: Joseph and Daniel. Both men were dreamers as well as interpreters. First, let's explore Joseph as a dreamer.

37 Now Jacob dwelt in the land where his father was a stranger, in the land of Canaan. ² This is the history of Joseph.

Joseph, being seventeen years old, was feeding the flock with his brothers. And the lad was with the sons of Bilhah and the sons of Zilpah, his father's wives; and Joseph brought a bad report of them to his father.

³ Now Israel loved Joseph more than all his children, because he was the son of his old age. Also he made him a tunic of many colors. ⁴ But when his brothers saw that their father loved him more than all his brothers, they hated him and could not speak peaceably to him.

⁵ Now Joseph had a dream, and he told it to his brothers; and they hated him even more. ⁶ So he said to them, "Please hear this dream which I have dreamed: ⁷ There we were, binding sheaves in the field. Then behold, my sheaf arose and also stood upright; and indeed your sheaves stood all around and bowed down to my sheaf."

⁸ And his brothers said to him, "Shall you indeed reign over us? Or shall you indeed have dominion over us?" So they hated him even more for his dreams and for his words.

⁹ Then he dreamed still another dream and told it to his brothers, and said, "Look, I have dreamed another dream. And this time, the sun, the moon, and the eleven stars bowed down to me."

¹⁰ So he told it to his father and his brothers; and his father rebuked him and said to him, "What is this dream that you have dreamed? Shall your mother and I and your brothers indeed come to bow down to the earth before you?" ¹¹ And his brothers envied him, but his father kept the matter in mind. (Gen. 37:1-11)

You are probably asking how Joseph knew what the symbols meant. In the Jewish culture, dreams were a common occurrence. Notice how the brothers knew what Joseph's dream meant, even though the interpretation is not mentioned. You know this because of their reaction.

* Underline verse 5: "And they hated him even more."

They were already jealous of their father's love for Joseph. Now God was talking to Joseph, and it made their jealousy grow.

* Look at verse 8.

They knew what the dream meant. They did not need to be told. In fact, they began to discuss the interpretation by asking Joseph, "Shall you reign over us?" Remember, Joseph was the youngest at this time. The youngest typically did not lead. The brothers knew what the dream meant, and it made them angry.

This point is made again with Joseph's second dream.

* Look at verse 10. Underline: "What is this dream that you have dreamed? Shall your mother and I and your brothers indeed come to bow down to the earth before you?"

Jacob knew what the dream meant. This leads you to understand that the Jewish people understood dreams. Remember that Jewish people are God's chosen people. God has talked with them since the time of Abraham. Their great-grandfather Abraham, their grandfather Isaac, and their father Jacob have all taught them how to hear the voice of God through many different means, dreams being one of them. Later in this study, we will discuss the meaning of symbols in dreams.

Let's look at Joseph as an interpreter. Remember, if God is speaking through a dream, He wants the dreamer to understand and to receive an interpret.

40 It came to pass after these things that the butler and the baker of the king of Egypt offended their lord, the king of Egypt. [2] And Pharaoh was angry with his two officers, the chief butler and the chief baker. [3] So he put them in custody in the house of the captain of the guard, in the prison, the place where Joseph was confined. [4] And the captain of the guard charged Joseph with them, and he served them; so they were in custody for a while.

[5] Then the butler and the baker of the king of Egypt, who were confined in the prison, had a dream, both of them, each man's dream in one night and each man's dream with its own interpretation. [6] And Joseph came in to them in the morning and looked at them, and saw that they were sad. [7] So he asked Pharaoh's officers who were with him in the custody of his lord's house, saying, "Why do you look so sad today?"

[8] And they said to him, "We each have had a dream, and there is no interpreter of it."

So Joseph said to them, "Do not interpretations belong to God? Tell them to me, please."

[9] Then the chief butler told his dream to Joseph, and said to him, "Behold, in my dream a vine was before me, [10] and in the vine were three branches; it was as though it budded, its blossoms shot forth, and its clusters brought forth ripe grapes. [11] Then Pharaoh's cup was in my hand; and I took the grapes and pressed them into Pharaoh's cup, and placed the cup in Pharaoh's hand."

[12] And Joseph said to him, "This is the interpretation of it: The three branches are three

days. [13] *Now within three days Pharaoh will lift up your head and restore you to your place, and you will put Pharaoh's cup in his hand according to the former manner, when you were his butler.* [14] *But remember me when it is well with you, and please show kindness to me; make mention of me to Pharaoh, and get me out of this house.* [15] *For indeed I was stolen away from the land of the Hebrews; and also I have done nothing here that they should put me into the dungeon."*

[16] *When the chief baker saw that the interpretation was good, he said to Joseph, "I also was in my dream, and there were three white baskets on my head.* [17] *In the uppermost basket were all kinds of baked goods for Pharaoh, and the birds ate them out of the basket on my head."*

[18] *So Joseph answered and said, "This is the interpretation of it: The three baskets are three days.* [19] *Within three days Pharaoh will lift off your head from you and hang you on a tree; and the birds will eat your flesh from you."*

[20] *Now it came to pass on the third day, which was Pharaoh's birthday, that he made a feast for all his servants; and he lifted up the head of the chief butler and of the chief baker among his servants.* [21] *Then he restored the chief butler to his butlership again, and he placed the cup in Pharaoh's hand.* [22] *But he hanged the chief baker, as Joseph had interpreted to them.* [23] *Yet the chief butler did not remember Joseph, but forgot him. (Gen. 40:1-23)*

* Underline verse 8.

Joseph is very quick to acknowledge that it is the Lord who gives interpretations. He is also confident that God will give him the interpretation. He understands that the Lord speaks to people through their dreams.

This is also a good example that we can ask others to help us interpret our dreams. There are times when a dream stirs up emotions and it is difficult to know the meaning.

Here is another example of Joseph interpreting a dream for another person besides himself.

41 Then it came to pass, at the end of two full years, that Pharaoh had a dream; and behold, he stood by the river. [2] *Suddenly there came up out of the river seven cows, fine looking and fat; and they fed in the meadow.* [3] *Then behold, seven other cows came up after them out of the river, ugly and gaunt, and stood by the other cows on the bank of the river.* [4] *And the ugly and gaunt cows ate up the seven fine looking and fat cows. So Pharaoh awoke.* [5] *He slept and dreamed a second time; and suddenly seven heads of grain came up on one stalk, plump and good.* [6] *Then behold, seven thin heads, blighted by the east wind, sprang up after them.* [7] *And the seven thin heads devoured the seven plump and full heads. So Pharaoh awoke, and indeed, it was a dream.* [8] *Now it came to pass in the morning that his spirit was troubled, and he sent and called for all the magicians of Egypt and all its wise men. And Pharaoh told them his dreams, but there was no one who could interpret them for Pharaoh.*

[9] *Then the chief butler spoke to Pharaoh, saying: "I remember my faults this day.* [10] *When Pharaoh was angry with his servants, and put me in custody in the house of the captain of the guard, both me and the chief baker,* [11] *we each had a dream in one night, he and I. Each of us dreamed according to the interpretation of his own dream.* [12] *Now there was a young Hebrew man with us there, a servant of the captain of the guard. And we told him, and he interpreted our dreams for us; to each man he interpreted according to his own dream.* [13] *And it came to pass, just as he interpreted for us, so it happened. He restored me to my office, and he hanged him."*

[14] *Then Pharaoh sent and called Joseph, and they brought him quickly out of the dungeon; and he shaved, changed his clothing, and came to Pharaoh.* [15] *And Pharaoh said to Joseph, "I have had a dream, and there is no one who can interpret it. But I have heard it said of you that you can understand a dream, to interpret it."*

[16] *So Joseph answered Pharaoh, saying, "It is not in me; God will give Pharaoh an answer of peace."*

[17] *Then Pharaoh said to Joseph: "Behold, in my dream I stood on the bank of the river.* [18] *Suddenly seven cows came up out of the river, fine looking and fat; and they fed in the meadow.* [19] *Then behold, seven other cows came up after them, poor and very ugly and gaunt, such ugliness as I have never seen in all the land of Egypt.* [20] *And the gaunt and ugly cows ate up the first seven, the fat cows.* [21] *When they had eaten them up, no one would have known that they had eaten them, for they were just as ugly as at the beginning. So I awoke.* [22] *Also I saw in my dream, and suddenly seven heads came up on one stalk, full and good.* [23] *Then behold, seven heads, withered, thin, and blighted by the east wind, sprang up after them.* [24] *And the thin heads devoured the seven good heads. So I told this to the magicians, but there was no one who could explain it to me."*

[25] *Then Joseph said to Pharaoh, "The dreams of Pharaoh are one; God has shown Pharaoh what He is about to do:* [26] *The seven good cows are seven years, and the seven good heads are seven years; the dreams are one.* [27] *And the seven thin and ugly cows which came up after them are seven years, and the seven empty heads blighted by the east wind are seven years of famine.* [28] *This is the thing which I have spoken to Pharaoh. God has shown Pharaoh what He is about to do.* [29] *Indeed seven years of great plenty will come throughout all the land of Egypt;* [30] *but after them seven years of famine will arise, and all the plenty will be forgotten in the land of Egypt; and the famine will deplete the land.* [31] *So the plenty will not be known in the land because of the famine following, for it will be very severe.* [32] *And the dream was repeated to Pharaoh twice because the thing is established by God, and God will shortly bring it to pass.*

[33] *"Now therefore, let Pharaoh select a discerning and wise man, and set him over the land of Egypt.* [34] *Let Pharaoh do this, and let him appoint officers over the land, to collect one-fifth of the produce of the land of Egypt in the seven plentiful years.* [35] *And let them gather all the food of those good years that are coming, and store up grain under the authority of Pharaoh, and let them keep food in the cities.* [36] *Then that food shall be as a*

reserve for the land for the seven years of famine which shall be in the land of Egypt that the land may not perish during the famine." (Gen. 41:1-36)

* Underline verse 16.

Joseph acknowledges once again that God is the one who gives the dream and therefore He is the one who has the interpretation.

Let's look at our second famous dreamer: Daniel.

7 In the first year of Belshazzar king of Babylon, Daniel had a dream and visions of his head while on his bed. Then he wrote down the dream, telling the main facts.

² Daniel spoke, saying, "I saw in my vision by night, and behold, the four winds of heaven were stirring up the Great Sea. ³ And four great beasts came up from the sea, each different from the other. ⁴ The first was like a lion, and had eagle's wings. I watched till its wings were plucked off; and it was lifted up from the earth and made to stand on two feet like a man, and a man's heart was given to it.

⁵ "And suddenly another beast, a second, like a bear. It was raised up on one side, and had three ribs in its mouth between its teeth. And they said thus to it: 'Arise, devour much flesh!'

⁶ "After this I looked, and there was another, like a leopard, which had on its back four wings of a bird. The beast also had four heads, and dominion was given to it.

⁷ "After this I saw in the night visions, and behold, a fourth beast, dreadful and terrible, exceedingly strong. It had huge iron teeth; it was devouring, breaking in pieces, and trampling the residue with its feet. It was different from all the beasts that were before it, and it had ten horns. ⁸ I was considering the horns, and there was another horn, a little one, coming up among them, before whom three of the first horns were plucked out by the roots. And there, in this horn, were eyes like the eyes of a man, and a mouth speaking pompous words.

⁹ "I watched till thrones were put in place,
And the Ancient of Days was seated;
His garment was white as snow,
And the hair of His head was like pure wool.
His throne was a fiery flame,
Its wheels a burning fire;
¹⁰ A fiery stream issued
And came forth from before Him.
A thousand thousands ministered to Him;

Ten thousand times ten thousand stood before Him.
The court was seated,
And the books were opened.

[11] *"I watched then because of the sound of the pompous words which the horn was speaking; I watched till the beast was slain, and its body destroyed and given to the burning flame.* [12] *As for the rest of the beasts, they had their dominion taken away, yet their lives were prolonged for a season and a time.*

[13] *"I was watching in the night visions,*
And behold, One like the Son of Man,
Coming with the clouds of heaven!
He came to the Ancient of Days,
And they brought Him near before Him.
[14] *Then to Him was given dominion and glory and a kingdom,*
That all peoples, nations, and languages should serve Him.
His dominion is an everlasting dominion,
Which shall not pass away,
And His kingdom the one
Which shall not be destroyed" (Dan. 7:1-14).

The above verses are Daniel's dream. The following verses tell us Daniel's reaction.

[15] *"I, Daniel, was grieved in my spirit within my body, and the visions of my head troubled me.* [16] *I came near to one of those who stood by, and asked him the truth of all this. So he told me and made known to me the interpretation of these things"* (Dan. 7:15-16).

It important to point out that this dream upset Daniel. Please note that your reaction to a dream does not discern if the dream is from God or the enemy. It is, however, important to note your emotions after a dream. Your emotions can help with the interpretation, but not the discernment of whom the dream is from.

Also note that God gave Daniel the interpretation because Daniel asked for it.

* Underline in verse 16: "and asked him the truth of all this. So he told me and made known to me the interpretations of these things."

How awesome and faithful is God! He speaks to you. He wants you to understand what He is telling you. Therefore, He will give you the interpretation.

Later in this study, I will discuss how to discern if a dream is from God or from the enemy. First, let's look at Daniel as an interpreter.

Nebuchadnezzar's Dream

2 *Now in the second year of Nebuchadnezzar's reign, Nebuchadnezzar had dreams; and his spirit was so troubled that his sleep left him.* [2] *Then the king gave the command to call the magicians, the astrologers, the sorcerers, and the Chaldeans to tell the king his dreams. So they came and stood before the king.* [3] *And the king said to them, "I have had a dream, and my spirit is anxious to know the dream."*

[4] *Then the Chaldeans spoke to the king in Aramaic,* [a] *"O king, live forever! Tell your servants the dream, and we will give the interpretation."*

[5] *The king answered and said to the Chaldeans, "My decision is firm: if you do not make known the dream to me, and its interpretation, you shall be cut in pieces, and your houses shall be made an ash heap.* [6] *However, if you tell the dream and its interpretation, you shall receive from me gifts, rewards, and great honor. Therefore tell me the dream and its interpretation."*

[7] *They answered again and said, "Let the king tell his servants the dream, and we will give its interpretation."*

[8] *The king answered and said, "I know for certain that you would gain time, because you see that my decision is firm:* [9] *if you do not make known the dream to me, there is only one decree for you! For you have agreed to speak lying and corrupt words before me till the time has changed. Therefore tell me the dream, and I shall know that you can give me its interpretation."*

[10] *The Chaldeans answered the king, and said, "There is not a man on earth who can tell the king's matter; therefore no king, lord, or ruler has ever asked such things of any magician, astrologer, or Chaldean.* [11] *It is a difficult thing that the king requests, and there is no other who can tell it to the king except the gods, whose dwelling is not with flesh."*

[12] *For this reason the king was angry and very furious, and gave the command to destroy all the wise men of Babylon.* [13] *So the decree went out, and they began killing the wise men; and they sought Daniel and his companions, to kill them.*

God Reveals Nebuchadnezzar's Dream

[14] *Then with counsel and wisdom Daniel answered Arioch, the captain of the king's guard, who had gone out to kill the wise men of Babylon;* [15] *he answered and said to Arioch the king's captain, "Why is the decree from the king so urgent?" Then Arioch made the decision known to Daniel.*

[16] *So Daniel went in and asked the king to give him time, that he might tell the king the interpretation.* [17] *Then Daniel went to his house, and made the decision known to Hananiah, Mishael, and Azariah, his companions,* [18] *that they might seek mercies from the God of heaven concerning this secret, so that Daniel and his companions might not*

perish with the rest of the wise men of Babylon. [19] Then the secret was revealed to Daniel in a night vision. So Daniel blessed the God of heaven.

[20] Daniel answered and said:

"Blessed be the name of God forever and ever,
For wisdom and might are His.
[21] And He changes the times and the seasons;
He removes kings and raises up kings;
He gives wisdom to the wise
And knowledge to those who have understanding.
[22] He reveals deep and secret things;
He knows what is in the darkness,
And light dwells with Him.
[23] "I thank You and praise You,
O God of my fathers;
You have given me wisdom and might,
And have now made known to me what we asked of You,
For You have made known to us the king's demand."

Daniel Explains the Dream

[24] Therefore Daniel went to Arioch, whom the king had appointed to destroy the wise men of Babylon. He went and said thus to him: "Do not destroy the wise men of Babylon; take me before the king, and I will tell the king the interpretation."

[25] Then Arioch quickly brought Daniel before the king, and said thus to him, "I have found a man of the captives of Judah, who will make known to the king the interpretation."

[26] The king answered and said to Daniel, whose name was Belteshazzar, "Are you able to make known to me the dream which I have seen, and its interpretation?"

[27] Daniel answered in the presence of the king, and said, "The secret which the king has demanded, the wise men, the astrologers, the magicians, and the soothsayers cannot declare to the king. [28] But there is a God in heaven who reveals secrets, and He has made known to King Nebuchadnezzar what will be in the latter days. Your dream, and the visions of your head upon your bed, were these: [29] As for you, O king, thoughts came to your mind while on your bed, about what would come to pass after this; and He who reveals secrets has made known to you what will be. [30] But as for me, this secret has not been revealed to me because I have more wisdom than anyone living, but for our sakes who make known the interpretation to the king, and that you may know the thoughts of your heart.

[31] "You, O king, were watching; and behold, a great image! This great image, whose splendor was excellent, stood before you; and its form was awesome. [32] This image's head

was of fine gold, its chest and arms of silver, its belly and thighs of bronze, [33] its legs of iron, its feet partly of iron and partly of clay. [34] You watched while a stone was cut out without hands, which struck the image on its feet of iron and clay, and broke them in pieces. [35] Then the iron, the clay, the bronze, the silver, and the gold were crushed together, and became like chaff from the summer threshing floors; the wind carried them away so that no trace of them was found. And the stone that struck the image became a great mountain and filled the whole earth.

[36] *"This is the dream. Now we will tell the interpretation of it before the king. [37] You, O king, are a king of kings. For the God of heaven has given you a kingdom, power, strength, and glory; [38] and wherever the children of men dwell, or the beasts of the field and the birds of the heaven, He has given them into your hand, and has made you ruler over them all— you are this head of gold. [39] But after you shall arise another kingdom inferior to yours; then another, a third kingdom of bronze, which shall rule over all the earth. [40] And the fourth kingdom shall be as strong as iron, inasmuch as iron breaks in pieces and shatters everything; and like iron that crushes, that kingdom will break in pieces and crush all the others. [41] Whereas you saw the feet and toes, partly of potter's clay and partly of iron, the kingdom shall be divided; yet the strength of the iron shall be in it, just as you saw the iron mixed with ceramic clay. [42] And as the toes of the feet were partly of iron and partly of clay, so the kingdom shall be partly strong and partly fragile. [43] As you saw iron mixed with ceramic clay, they will mingle with the seed of men; but they will not adhere to one another, just as iron does not mix with clay. [44] And in the days of these kings the God of heaven will set up a kingdom which shall never be destroyed; and the kingdom shall not be left to other people; it shall break in pieces and consume all these kingdoms, and it shall stand forever. [45] Inasmuch as you saw that the stone was cut out of the mountain without hands, and that it broke in pieces the iron, the bronze, the clay, the silver, and the gold—the great God has made known to the king what will come to pass after this. The dream is certain, and its interpretation is sure."(Dan. 2:1-45)*

Again, I want to point out that this dream bothered Nebuchadnezzar. It is not uncommon for a dream to move you emotionally. In your journaling of your dreams, take note of your emotions after a dream. God will use your emotions to further speak to you.

Also, Daniel had to ask God for the interpretation.

* Underline Daniel 2:17-19.

All interpretations come from God. This confirms Joseph's comment when he was asked to interpret Pharaoh's dream. All interpretations come from God.

It is important to emphasize that God gives you a dream because He wants to talk to you. Therefore as you seek Him for meaning, He will give you the interpretation. Be patient if you don't get the answer right away. As a teacher, I know that you will learn a topic more in depth if I give you a puzzle to figure out or a question to ponder. God works the same way. If He just spewed out facts and information, you may not consider the information as seriously as you ought. Take the teachings of Jesus. Often He used parables to teach the people. When Jesus and the disciples were alone, the disciples would ask, "What do the parables mean?" Notice, they were alone with Jesus. They talked with Jesus. They listened to Jesus. If you don't understand a dream, take time to ask questions and listen to what your loving Savior wants to teach you.

Look at Daniel 2:17. *Write down what Daniel did.

Daniel asked his friends to pray and ask God to give the interpretation of the dream. There may be times that you will need to ask a friend what they believe the interpretation to be. I have often done this. A dream may have upset me, and because I do not have peace, I do not get the interpretation. I could not hear from God. (I discuss the importance of peace in order to hear in great detail in *How to Hear God's Voice; Intro to Prophecy*.) Again, dreams can move you emotionally, so it is okay to ask a friend for help in discerning God's interpretation.

Let's take a look at other dreams in scripture. Note the first sets of dreamers are believers, one from the Old Testament and one from the New Testament. The second sets of dreamers are unbelievers, one from the Old Testament and one from the New Testament.

Believers:

Jacob

[12] "*Then he dreamed, and behold, a ladder was set up on the earth, and its top reached to heaven; and there the angels of God were ascending and descending on it.*"(Gen. 28:12).

Joseph (Mary's husband)

[20] *But while he thought about these things, behold, an angel of the Lord appeared to him in a dream, saying, "Joseph, son of David, do not be afraid to take to you Mary your wife, for that which is conceived in her is of the Holy Spirit.* [21] *And she will bring forth a Son, and you shall call His name JESUS, for He will save His people from their sins*"(Matt. 1:20-21).
[13] "*Now when they had departed, behold, an angel of the Lord appeared to Joseph in a dream, saying, 'Arise, take the young Child and His mother, flee to Egypt, and stay there until I bring you word; for Herod will seek the young Child to destroy Him'.*"(Matt.2:13).
[19] "*Now when Herod was dead, behold, an angel of the Lord appeared in a dream to Joseph*

in Egypt, [20] *saying, 'Arise, take the young Child and His mother, and go to the land of Israel, for those who sought the young Child's life are dead.'* [21] *Then he arose, took the young Child and His mother, and came into the land of Israel.*

[22] *But when he heard that Archelaus was reigning over Judea instead of his father Herod, he was afraid to go there. And being warned by God in a dream, he turned aside into the region of Galilee.* [23] *And he came and dwelt in a city called Nazareth, that it might be fulfilled which was spoken by the prophets, 'He shall be called a Nazarene'"(Matt. 2:19-23).*

Unbelievers:

Abimelech

"[3] *But God came to Abimelech in a dream by night, and said to him, 'Indeed you are a dead man because of the woman whom you have taken, for she is a man's wife'"(Gen. 20:3).*

Pilate's wife

[19] "*While he was sitting on the judgment seat, his wife sent to him, saying, 'Have nothing to do with that just Man, for I have suffered many things today in a dream because of Him'"(Matt. 27:19).*

I find this extremely interesting. The Word tells us that God is a respecter of no man (see Romans 2:11). This includes dreams. God will give dreams to believers as well as nonbelievers. What is so cool about dreams is that when you have a dream, your conscience is out of the way. You cannot argue with God like you can with a prophecy. You're sleeping! The same is true with a nonbeliever. God can talk to them without them arguing back.

Also notice how personal and intimate dreams are. In many cases, a dream shakes a nonbeliever to their very soul. God is trying to get their attention!

You have looked at examples of people having dreams. Let's look at what the Bible says about dreams and the purpose of dreams.

[15] *In a dream, in a vision of the night,*
When deep sleep falls upon men,
While slumbering on their beds,

16 Then He opens the ears of men,
And seals their instruction.
17 In order to turn man from his deed,
And conceal pride from man,
18 He keeps back his soul from the Pit,
And his life from perishing by the sword. (Job 33:15-18)

* Underline verse 16. What is the purpose of a dream?

6 Then He said,
"Hear now My words:
If there is a prophet among you,
I, the LORD, MAKE MYSELF KNOWN TO HIM IN A VISION;
I speak to him in a dream. " (Num. 12:6)

* What is the purpose of a dream?

28 "And it shall come to pass afterward
That I will pour out My Spirit on all flesh;
Your sons and your daughters shall prophesy,
Your old men shall dream dreams,
Your young men shall see visions." (Joel 2:28)

* Who is God going to give His Spirit to?

* Does age or gender matter?

_____

Journal Week One:

This week I want you to write down any dreams that you remember. It does not matter if it was just one item or one number. It is important to start practicing. As you get ready to go to bed, put a notebook or journal close to your bed, along with a writing utensil. As soon as you sit up in bed, write what you remember. Because you are just beginning, it will be easy to forget. Write it down as soon as you can.

Also, before you fall asleep, ask God to speak to you through a dream. It is a time to speak to God about your desire to hear from Him and to grow closer to Him. After you are finished asking God to speak to you, spend time praising and adoring God. If you have difficulty in this, read a Psalm that speaks of God's goodness.

These are just a few things to do to prepare you to dream. Remember to write down whatever you remember, no matter how minimal it may seem to you.

Dream 1

Dream 2

Dream 3

Dream 4

Dream 5

HOW TO HEAR GOD'S VOICE: INTRO TO DREAM INTERPRETATION WEEK TWO

DREAMS ARE SCRIPTURAL AND A way that God speaks to you. Dreams are given by God to people of every age and every gender; everyone can receive dreams. However, there is a deceiver out there called Satan. He can also give dreams. Another way that dreams may come is if there is something you are thinking about, something you are obsessing about; it can manifest in your dreams. How do you know who the dream comes from?

In this chapter we will discuss these questions:

Where do dreams come from?
How do you discern where the dream comes from? In other words: What is the source of the dream?
How do you know if the dream is about you or the person you are dreaming about?

Dreams can come from many sources. I have had terrible dreams after having food that was way too spicy and eaten way too late at night. On the other hand, I have had very meaningful dreams from God. In addition to that, I have had dreams about things that I have been thinking about or worrying about. How do I tell who the sources of my dreams are?

I am going to make a statement and then walk you through the scriptures to explain my thought process. Statement: Dreams with color are from God, and dreams in black and white (absence of color) are from Satan.

Let's first compare light with darkness. When you are in the light or in full sunlight, do you see colors? Yes. If you are in the dark, what do you see? You see shades of grey, and black and white. I have learned through classes, books, and experiences that when I have a dream in color, it comes from God. If I have a dream in black and white, it is usually from Satan.

In these next series of verses I want you to look at the comparison of good to evil. It is always accompanied with a comparison of light to dark. As you read through these scriptures, circle the words "good" and "light" (or any form of the word) and underline the words "evil", "bad" and "dark" (or any form of the word). Do you notice the comparison?

"But when I looked for good, evil came to me; And when I waited for light, then came darkness" (Job 30:26).

"For You will light my lamp; The Lord my God will enlighten my darkness" (Ps. 18:28).

"The lamp of the body is the eye. Therefore, when your eye is good, your whole body also is full of light. But when your eye is bad, your body also is full of darkness" (Luke 11:34).

"And this is the condemnation, that the light has come into the world, and men loved darkness rather than light, because their deeds were evil"(John 3:19).

"Then Jesus spoke to them again, saying, 'I am the light of the world. He who follows Me shall not walk in darkness, but have the light of life'" (John 8:12).

"Then Jesus said to them, 'A little while longer the light is with you. Walk while you have the light, lest darkness overtake you; he who walks in darkness does not know where he is going'" (John 12:35).

[17] *"'I will [a]deliver you from the Jewish people, as well as from the Gentiles, to whom I [b] now send you,* [18] *to open their eyes, in order to turn them from darkness to light, and from the power of Satan to God, that they may receive forgiveness of sins and an inheritance among those who are sanctified[c] by faith in Me'"(Acts 26:17-18).*

"For you were once darkness, but now you are light in the Lord. Walk as children of light" (Eph.5:8).

"This is the message which we have heard from Him and declare to you, that God is light and in Him is no darkness at all" (John 1:5).

Do you see the relationship between light and good? Do you see the relationship between dark and evil?

* Who refers to Himself as good?

In the light you can see colors; therefore, you can conclude that when you have a dream in color, it is from God.

* What is the opposite of light?

* What is the opposite of good?
* Therefore, who is opposite of good; opposite of God? Who is evil?

In the dark, you cannot see light. You see gray and black and white. Therefore, you can conclude that a dream in black and white is not from God, and therefore, the dream is from Satan. It is possible that you have a dream with only one color. As long as there is one color, consider the dream to be from God. In the case where there is only one color, that color will have a specific meaning that God is trying to communicate to you about. However, at this point we are trying to discern the source of the dream; who is the dream from? Therefore, we are just concerned about if the dream is in color or black and white.

There is another source which dreams can come from: the dreamer. You, as a dreamer, can cause yourself to dream.

> [3] *For a dream comes through much activity,*
> *And a fool's voice is known by his many words. (Eccel. 5:3)*

If you are obsessing about a subject, you can force yourself to dream about it. Let me explain. I was in the process of writing this Bible study. I was having a tough time disciplining myself to just sit down and write! One afternoon, a free afternoon, I decided to take a nap instead of writing. Guess what I dreamed about--writing. I woke up thinking, "All right, all right, I will sit down and write." You often will dream about something that is weighing heavily on your mind.

When you are worrying or obsessing about something, you must be aware that it can affect your dream life. One way to deal with this is to take time before you go to sleep to give God your concerns. He knows what is going on already.

Please take note: there is a difference between obsessing verses thinking or pondering about something. Obsessing is a place of worrying and fretting. One can ponder and yet have peace. Only you know if you have crossed the line of pondering into a place of worry.

Let's take a look at Jeremiah 29. This is a great example of God speaking to the people of Israel about their dreams.

> *Now these are the words of the letter that Jeremiah the prophet sent from Jerusalem to the remainder of the elders who were carried away captive—to the priests, the prophets, and all the people whom Nebuchadnezzar had carried away captive from Jerusalem to Babylon.* [2] *(This happened after Jeconiah the king, the queen mother, the eunuchs, the princes of Judah and Jerusalem, the craftsmen, and the smiths had departed from Jerusalem.)* [3] *The letter was sent by the hand of Elasah the son of Shaphan, and Gemariah the son of Hilkiah, whom Zedekiah king of Judah sent to Babylon, to Nebuchadnezzar king of Babylon, saying,*
> [4]*" Thus says the LORD OF HOSTS, THE GOD OF ISRAEL, TO ALL WHO WERE CARRIED AWAY CAPTIVE, WHOM I HAVE CAUSED TO BE CARRIED AWAY FROM JERUSALEM TO BABYLON:*

5" Build houses and dwell in them; plant gardens and eat their fruit. ⁶ Take wives and beget sons and daughters; and take wives for your sons and give your daughters to husbands, so that they may bear sons and daughters—that you may be increased there, and not diminished. ⁷ And seek the peace of the city where I have caused you to be carried away captive, and pray to the LORD FOR IT; FOR IN ITS PEACE YOU WILL HAVE PEACE. ⁸ For thus says the LORD OF HOSTS, THE GOD OF ISRAEL: DO NOT LET YOUR PROPHETS AND YOUR DIVINERS WHO ARE IN YOUR MIDST DECEIVE YOU, NOR LISTEN TO YOUR DREAMS WHICH YOU CAUSE TO BE DREAMED. ⁹ For they prophesy falsely to you in My name; I have not sent them, says the LORD." (JEREMIAH 29:1-9)

The Israelites have been taken into captivity. They are worried about their future and what God has for them. They have sought the advice of the prophets. God is warning them not to listen to their dreams, because all of their worrying has caused the people to dream false dreams.

* Look at verse 8. Underline "nor listen to your dreams which you cause to be dreamed."

The Israelites were worrying and fretting about the situation they were in. They were going to the prophets and asking what they should do. They were asking the prophets what their dreams meant. However, God was telling them that their worrying was causing the dreams.

God is good. When we release our worries and concerns to Him, He will encourage us.

10" For thus says the LORD: AFTER SEVENTY YEARS ARE COMPLETED AT BABYLON, I WILL VISIT YOU AND PERFORM MY GOOD WORD TOWARD YOU, AND CAUSE YOU TO RETURN TO THIS PLACE. ¹¹ For I know the thoughts that I think toward you, says the LORD, THOUGHTS OF PEACE AND NOT OF EVIL, TO GIVE YOU A FUTURE AND A HOPE. ¹² Then you will call upon Me and go and pray to Me, and I will listen to you. ¹³ And you will seek Me and find Me, when you search for Me with all your heart. ¹⁴ I will be found by you, says the LORD, AND I WILL BRING YOU BACK FROM YOUR CAPTIVITY; I WILL GATHER YOU FROM ALL THE NATIONS AND FROM ALL THE PLACES WHERE I HAVE DRIVEN YOU, SAYS THE LORD, AND I WILL BRING YOU TO THE PLACE FROM WHICH I CAUSE YOU TO BE CARRIED AWAY CAPTIVE." (JEREMIAH 29:1-14)

* Underline verse 11.

God wants to encourage the Israelites that they will go through challenges, but He has good plans for them. God also encourages them to seek Him. Not a prophet, but Him; He wants to be the one the Israelites turn to. He wants to give them hope and direction.

Let's return to the question: "How do you know who the dream comes from? Who is the source of the dream?"

When I interpret a dream, I have to check my heart: am I worrying or obsessing about something that may affect my dream? A good practice before I go to sleep is to give my worries and concerns to God. It will eliminate the possibility that I am the source of the dream.

So when I have a dream, I ask myself a couple of questions. "Am I worrying about something?"

If the answer is Yes, I am worrying; I need to talk to God about the subject and consider the dream my imagination.

If the answer is No, I am not worrying; I can eliminate myself as a possible source of the dream.

The next question I ask is, "Is there any color in my dream?"

If the dream has color, it is from God.

If the dream is in black and white, it is from Satan.

Please note: you may only remember one color of one object. That is still a dream having color, and you can conclude that it is from God. If that happens, that object and that color are definitely important and noteworthy.

___

Let's discuss how to know if a dream is about you (the dreamer) or the person in your dream.

___

To determine if the dream is about you or the person in the dream; ask yourself this question: Am I active, or am I observing in my dream?

Let me explain.

When you are dreaming and you are part of the dream, or active, the dream is about you. God is using the other people in the dream to relay a message. I will explain more in a later chapter.

When you are not a part of the dream, or rather you are observing, the dream is not about you. God is talking to you about someone. He is asking you to pray for the person in the dream.

Example: My daughter had a dream about a friend who was cutting. In reality, she knew her friend did not cut; however, in the dream, her friend was cutting. My daughter was not in the dream. She was observing her friend cutting.

When interpreting a dream, the question to ask is, "Was my daughter, the dreamer, active in the dream or observing?" In this case, my daughter was observing. Therefore, my daughter's dream was not about her. The dream was about my daughter's friend. God was asking my daughter to pray for her friend, that the friend would not cut herself. Studies have shown that kids cut themselves due to anxiety and pressure and inner pain. My daughter and I prayed for her friend to have peace and comfort and find ways to deal with her anxiety that would not be self-harming.

It is important to decipher if you are an active character in the dream or not. The majority of the time, you will be the main character in your dream. You will be active in your dream. God is speaking to you about you. Therefore, the others in the dream are ways God is trying to speak to you. You must look at the people in your dream as symbols, not literally.

If you are observing the dream, the dream is about the person in the dream. These dreams are called Intercession dreams. God trusts you to pray for the person in your dream. He is giving you clues in the dream about how to pray for the person. When my daughter had a dream about her friend, she was observing; therefore the dream was about her friend. We asked God how to pray for her friend, and the dream gave us clues.

These types of dreams will often be given to leaders who oversee others. For example, a mother can have a dream about her child. If she is observing in the dream, God is asking her to pray for her child. A pastor may have dreams about members in his congregation. God is asking him to pray for those members. Your spiritual gift may be intercession. You may have dreams in which you observe situations. God is asking you to pray for those situations. Be careful to ask God how He wants you to pray.

Remember, 99 percent of your dreams are about you. Only if you are observing is the dream about someone else.

Let's recap: There is space provided for you to write down your answers.
Who can dream?

Who are possible sources of a dream? Who can give dreams? Where do dreams come from? There are three possibilities.

How do you discern the source of the dream?

How do you know if the dream is about you or the person you are dreaming about?

The answers to these questions are available after the Journal Week Two section.

Journal Week Two

Last week I gave you three things to do to prepare to dream. What were they?
1.

2.

3.

This week I would like you to take two more steps to prepare for your dream.
1. Turn off technology/electronics a significant amount of time before you go to bed. It may be twenty minutes, or it may be an hour. You have to judge how much time you spend on technology/electronics.
2. Spend some time talking to God about things that are bothering you. Spend time repenting for worrying and not trusting God with these situations. Spend time repenting of anything that needs to be taken care of. This is especially important so that you eliminate yourself as the source of a dream.

Write down any colors or numbers that you wrote down in your dream journal from last week.

1.

2.

3.

4.

5.

(We will discuss the meanings of colors and numbers in the next chapter. You can write the meaning to these colors/numbers after the lesson.)

Again this week, I want you to write down any dreams that you remember. It does not matter if it was just one item or one number. It is important to keep practicing.

Dream 1

Dream 2

Dream 3

Dream 4

Dream 5

Answers to questions in Week Two section:

Who can dream? Everyone

Who are the possible sources of a dream? God, Satan, the dreamer

How do you discern the source of the dream? First, check your heart. Are you worrying about something? If yes, you are the source. Second, is there color? If yes, God is the source. If no, Satan is the source.

How do you know if the dream is about the dreamer or a person in the dream? Is the dreamer active or observing in the dream? If active, the dream is about the dreamer. If observing, the dream is about the person in the dream.

DEBORAH SANDOW

How to Hear God's Voice: Intro to Dream Interpretation Week Three

THIS WEEK WE WILL BEGIN to talk about dream language. Please realize that dreams are God's way of talking to you. He wants to develop a relationship with you, so He gives you a dream or a puzzle to figure out. He uses people, symbols, and objects which He knows mean something to you. For example, my family was very active in softball. I joke about the fact that a ball was put in my hand before I could walk. I often have dreams about playing ball. I know what God is saying to me because it is so personal. My husband loves war games and war movies. God often talks to him through war or military scenes. My husband understands military strategies, and so he knows what God is trying to say to him. God knows you so intimately that He knows what you will relate to. Dreams are very personal.

With that being said, there is no recipe for interpreting dreams. God wants to talk to you. He wants to develop a relationship with you, so a certain color won't always mean the same thing; a particular animal won't always mean the same thing. That is why it is important to develop a dream language that God has used with you. So as we discuss the meanings of different colors, people, and objects, write down what God is telling you. Also stay open to the fact that God may add to that dream language as you grow in your gift of interpreting.

Let's begin with colors.

Dream Language: Colors

Have you ever had a dream in full technicolor?
Have you have had a dream where you can only remember the color of one specific item? What was that color?

In the Bible study *How to Hear God's Voice; Intro to Prophecy,* we discuss the meanings of color. Here is an excerpt of that study.

God can also talk to us through colors. There are many colors spoken of in the Bible that have a particular meaning. One of the most memorable times God used colors was after the flood. God set a rainbow in the sky. This rainbow was the full color wheel. It represented the promise of God, a covenant that God made with man (Gen. 9). Whenever I see a rainbow, I think about the promises that God has made in His word, the promises He has spoken to my heart; and I am encouraged.

As we look at colors, think about the natural attitudes or emotions they evoke. Think about what they might represent. Let's start with an easy one. . . What do you think of when you see the color red.? . . . Love, hearts, warmth . . . Are there negative feelings associated with red? . . . Anger, war.

In scripture, red usually refers to blood. It is the blood of Jesus that cleanses us from all unrighteousness (1 John 1:7). Think about that: Jesus showed us tremendous love by dying and shedding His blood. Think about the war He faced as He was tempted in the Garden of Gethsemane. Are you beginning to see how colors are scriptural, and how God can use colors to talk to you?

This leads me to a major point: Listening to God is about developing your relationship with God. How do you develop a relationship? You talk back and forth. When God shows you a color, ask Him what He is trying to tell you. There are positive and negatives to everything. So talk to God and listen to what He is revealing to you.

Let's try another . . . What do you think of when you see blue? Sky, water, heaven . . . In Ezekiel, the blue stone sapphire is often used to describe heaven. Blue can also mean God is trying to lift you up; He is trying to give you new revelation or understanding of who God is. He is bringing you to a higher level with God. In the scriptures, blue represents God revealed.

"They saw the God of Israel. And there was under His feet as it were a paved work of sapphire stone, and it was like the very heavens in its clarity" (Exod. 24:10).

In this story, Moses had taken the elders up the mountain to meet with God. It was there that the elders had a greater revelation of who God is. Therefore, blue can mean revelation.

This leads me to another major point: Everything you hear must line up with the Word of God! Even the things I teach you. Everything I teach had better have a scripture to back it up. Everything you hear in your journaling time needs to have a scripture to back it up. Testing the spirits is crucial, and the scripture is your measuring stick.

Let's try another . . . What do you think of when you see purple? . . . Royalty . . . Jesus was dressed in a purple robe (John 19:2-3). Daniel was dressed in purple when he was honored (Daniel 5:29).

For convenience, I use a book to help me find meaning of colors: The Symbolic Meanings of Colors by Rose Crownover.

Let's dig into the topic of colors in more depth.

Many colors have an emotional connotation to them. Green: you may think of jealousy, the green-eyed monster; red: you may think of love or Valentine's Day; blue: you may think of someone being depressed or sad. Each color has a positive and a negative meaning. For the color green, negative is jealousy; positive is growth. (Think of plants: they are healthiest and growing when they are green.) For red, negative is anger; positive is love. (Think of the saying, "I am so angry I am seeing red.") For blue, negative is sad or feeling down; positive is God wants to lift you up toward the blue sky and reveal things to you--revelation.

So as you are interpreting a dream, remember, a dream is a puzzle that God has given you to grow your relationship with Him. Ask Him if the interpretation of the color is using the negative or positive meaning of the color. God wants to develop your communication with Him. I have given you a few examples to use as a springboard into other possibilities.

* What is the predominate color in fire?
* Does God represent Himself as fire?

"God is a consuming fire" (Heb. 12:29).

Red could possibly mean fire. Orange, blue, or white could possibly mean fire. These colors are all in fire.

Let's look at Ezekiel:

[12] *And by the river upon the bank thereof, on this side and on that side, shall grow all trees for meat, whose leaf shall not fade, neither shall the fruit thereof be consumed: it shall bring forth new fruit according to his months, because their waters they issued out of the sanctuary: and the fruit thereof shall be for meat, and the leaf thereof for medicine. (Ezek. 47:12 King James Version)*

What color are leaves?
* Underline the last phrase "the leaf thereof for medicine." What were they using the leaf for in this verse?
Green could represent healing.
Isn't this fun? God is so creative. He is a God of color and wonder and creativity. Dreams are a fun puzzle to speak to you in a creative way.

[2] *"He makes me to lie down in green pastures; He leads me beside the still waters" (Ps.23:2).*

* What is green in this scripture?
* What is David saying that the Lord made him do?

* Is it possible for the color green to mean rest?
Let's look at some more scriptures.

2 *"And the soldiers twisted a crown of thorns and put it on His head, and they put on Him a purple robe. 3 Then they said, 'Hail, King of the Jews!' And they struck Him with their hands"(John 19:2-3).*

29 *"Then Belshazzar gave the command, and they clothed Daniel with purple and put a chain of gold around his neck, and made a proclamation concerning him that he should be the third ruler in the kingdom"(Dan. 5:29).*

* What color was mentioned in both of these scriptures?

* When purple garments were put on both men, what did it signify?

* What does the color purple represent?

Remember, there is no recipe for interpreting dreams. I am giving you some basics to help you get started. Dream interpretation uses allegories to help explain. You have to think symbolically and not literally. There are always things in a dream that need to be interpreted, and not taken at face value. When considering the colors of your dream, the most important thing to discern is, "Does my dream have color or is it black and white?" Remember, this helps discern the source of the dream. If one specific color may not stick out, but you know there was color, the dream source is God. If there is one specific color, seek God for understanding of the color.

Here is a chart of colors to get you started. This chart tells the most common meanings. Like you have discovered, there are many meanings to each color. As you dream, ask God for the interpretation. I've given you an APPENDIX OF DREAM LANGUAGE at the end of the study; add the meanings of colors to this appendix as God gives new ones to you. Be sure and ask God to confirm it to you with a scripture. He always will. It is like a treasure hunt between you and God, and it will grow your knowledge of scriptures.

White (+) Spirit of the Lord, holy power; (-) religious spirit

Red (+) wisdom, anointing, power; (-) anger, war

Green (+) conscience, growth, prosperity; (-) envy, jealousy, pride

Blue (+) communion, revelation; (-) depression, sorrow, anxiety

Yellow (+) mind, hope, gift of God; (-) fear, coward, intellectual pride

Orange (+) perseverance; (-) stubbornness, strong-minded

Purple (+) authority, royalty; (-) false authority, licentiousness

As you read your Bible, write down scriptures that mention colors. Can you confirm the meanings of the colors mentioned above? I bet you can! Have fun treasure hunting. Write down your discoveries.

Dream Language: Numbers

There are times that a number will stick out in a dream. Maybe you had five babies in your dream. Or you remember there were two doors into a room. Somehow a detail will stick out that has to do with a number. Maybe you were buying something in a dream, and it cost seven dollars.

Interestingly, all Hebrew letters have a word meaning and a numerical meaning. Numbers are very important. The Bible is full of numbers, in fact there is a book called Numbers. God will use numbers to talk to you in a dream.

A rule when interpreting the meaning of a number is to look in the bible where the number was first used. For instance, the number four was first used when describing the activities of creation on day four. What was happening? It was the day when God created all the animals, the plants, the birds of the air, and the fish of the sea. Therefore, number four means "creative works." Think about the number seven. What happened on day seven of creation? Everything was completed. The number seven often means completion. Examine the number eight. What happened on day eight? It was a new beginning of a new planet, the beginning of time. So, the number eight means "new beginnings."

Some numbers require a little digging into the Word of God, some investigation. Let's take the number eleven. When is it first used in the Bible?

*"And he (Jacob) arose that night and took his two wives, his two female servants, and his **eleven** sons, and crossed over the ford of Jabbok" (Gen. 32:22 emphasis added).*

At this point of Jacob's life, he had recently left his father-in-law's house. Jacob was about to meet his brother Easu for the first time since he had tricked their father into giving himself Esau's blessing. He was frightened that his brother was going to kill him. He had spent time sending his flock and servants ahead of him as a peace offering. He was about to cross over and meet his brother face to face. He sent his wives and eleven sons ahead of himself, and he was left alone. He was visited by a man who we later learn is an angel. The two of them wrestled.

Jacob's hip was damaged in the encounter. The angel asked to be released, and Jacob replied, "Not until you bless me." The angel asked "What is your name?" Jacob responded and the angel replied, "No longer will your name be Jacob, but Israel" (see Gen. 32).

Here we see Jacob going through many transitions. He has left the demands of working for his father-in-law. He is seeing a brother for the first time that he tricked many years ago. He has just wrestled with an angel and received an injury that will forever give him a limp. But more importantly, he has received a new name, a new identity.

From all these events and the fact that this is the first usage of the number eleven, we can surmise that the number eleven means "transition."

Another situation where eleven can be understood as meaning transition is in the situation right after Jesus' ascension. The disciples were in a transition. They had not only lost Jesus, but they had lost one of the disciples and they were down to eleven. They were in a huge transition. "What do we do? We have lost our leader Jesus, and we have lost one of our own, Judas."

Let's start at the beginning. Here's is a chart of sorts. At the back of this study, I have created an appendix. It has this list repeated and space for you to add meanings as you grow in your dream language with God. Remember you can add to this list when you find a scripture or when God gives you revelation on its meaning. There is no recipe.

Number one means "God." There is one true God.

Number two means "witness." *By the mouth of two or three witnesses a matter shall be established" (Deut. 19:15).*

Number three means "God." We believe in the triune God.

Number four means "creative works."

Number five means "grace."

Number six means "man." (Man was created on the sixth day.) It can also mean "double." (The Israelites were told to collect double portions of the manna on the sixth day.)

Number seven means "completion."

Number eight means "new beginnings."

Number nine means "fullness." (There are nine fruits of the spirit.)

Number ten means "journey," "trials," and "testing." (Daniel asked for a ten-day trial of what they wanted to eat. See Dan. 1:12, 14.)

Number eleven means "transition" (discussed earlier).

Number twelve means "government." (There were twelve tribes of Judah and there were twelve disciples.)

What do you do if you have a complex number like fifty-six?

There are different things you can do to interpret a complex number. Remember there is no recipe. This is God's way of talking to you, and He will use creative ways to communicate. Ask God which method to use when interpreting complex numbers.

One way to handle a number like fifty-six is to look at each number. Fifty-six could mean five(grace) and six(double). God wants to give you double grace.

One way to look at fifty-six is to add the numbers together: 5+6=11. God is trying to tell you that you are in a transition.

One way is to look at the factors of fifty-six: 7x8=56. Seven means "completion" and eight means "new beginnings." God may be telling you that this season is completed, and you are about to begin something new or a new season.

Remember, God is a creative God. When you have a complex number, ask God how He is talking to you through this number. You will know, because you will have a witness in your heart. You will have a gut feeling that tells you, "Yes, that's it."

Here are a few more numbers that are common.

Thirteen--rebellion
Fourteen--double anointing (double seven)
Fifteen--mercy, reprieve
Sixteen--established new beginnings (double eight)
Seventeen--elect of God (Joseph was 17en when he had his dreams from God.)
Thirty--begin ministry (Jesus was thirty when He began his ministry.)
Forty--testing (Israelites walked around the wilderness for forty years)
Fifty--jubilee, debt cancelation
One hundred--Child of Promise, fruitfulness, promise fulfilled (Isaac was born when Abraham was one hundred years old)

As you read your Bible, write down scriptures that mention numbers. Can you confirm the meanings for the above numbers? Start writing down the meanings you discover in the appendix found at the end of this study. This enables you to recall the way God has spoken to you in the past, so the next time you have that number in a dream, you can refer to it.

Let's try interpreting a couple of dreams. Remember to pull out important facts: colors, and numbers. The answers will be provided after the journal entries.

Dream 1: My daughter had a stack of money: one hundred-, fifty-, and one-dollar bills. She counted it and gave it to me. I was looking and counting through the stack of money.

The first question we have to ask is:"Is there any color, or is the dream in black and white?" It's possible you don't remember any specific color, but you will know if it has color. A black-

and-white dream is very obvious. If there is color, the source of the dream is God. If the dream is in black and white, the source of the dream is Satan. As the dreamer, I recall there was color. Therefore, the dream was from God.

The second question to ask, as the dreamer, is: am I active or observing the dream? In this dream I am active, I was given the money, and I am counting and looking at the money. Therefore, the dream is about me.

What are the important details?
    1 My daughter
    2 One hundred
    3 Fifty
    4 One

What are the meanings of the details?
    1 My daughter means gifting or callings. (This will be explained in later chapters.)
    2 One hundred--promises fulfilled
    3 Fifty--jubilee or debt canceled
    4 One--God

Using the meanings of the details, write a one or two-sentence interpretation.

"God wants me to know that He is fulfilling His promises concerning my gifts and callings and my debt."

Let's try another one. I am going to leave the questions blank to give you an opportunity to try to write out the interpretation. The answers are found after the Journal Week Three. This will be the pattern from now on when we practice interpreting dreams.

Dream 2: I am walking in shoes with purple laces.

I have said that there are no recipes for interpretation of dreams. However, there is a process. First, the source of the dream must be determined. Second, who the dream is about (the dreamer or the person in the dream) must be determined. Then, looking at the details of the dream, an interpretation is developed.

First question: Is there color, or is the dream in black-and-white? Who is the source of the dream?

Second question: is the dreamer active or observing in the dream? Who is the dream about?

What are the details?

1.
2.

What do the details mean?
1.
2.

Using the meanings of the details, write a one-to-two sentence interpretation.

Journal Week Three:

We have discussed how to prepare to dream. Write down those preparations.

1.

2.

3.

4.

5.

Let's add to this list of preparation.
1. Add a time of praying a hedge of protection (see Job 1:10, Ps. 129:5) and asking God to place His angels all around you (see Ps.91).
2. Spend time reading scriptures, and ask God to speak to you through the scriptures.

Look up the colors and numbers that have been in your dreams. Add them to the appendix in the back. Continue to add colors and numbers as your dream life increases. You are starting your own personal dream language with God.

Again this week, I want you to write down any dreams that you remember. It does not matter if it was just one item or one number. It is important to keep practicing.

Dream 1

Dream 2

Dream 3

Dream 4

Dream 5

Choose one of your dreams to write in a circle. Writing the dream in a circle will unlock your mind to think outside the box. It will help you to think about the dream in a symbolic way. Another way to try unlocking your brain is to turn the page upside-down and write the dream on the upside down page. A third method for unlocking your brain is to turn the page on its side and write the dream sideways or at a diagonal. Try one or two of these methods.

"Did you receive an interpretation? Write it down."

"Write a prayer of thanksgiving for the interpretation."

Start a list of animals, people, or objects that have been in your dream.

1.

2.

3.

4.

5.

(We will discuss the meanings of animals, people, and objects in the next chapter. You can write the meaning to these animals/people/objects after the lesson)

Answers to Interpretation Practice:

Dream 2
>First Question: There is color; therefore, God is the source.
>Second Question: The dreamer is active; therefore, the dream is about the dreamer.

What are the details?
1. Shoes
2. Purple

What do the details represent?
1. Shoes--walking, the path the dreamer is on
2. Purple--authority, royalty

Using the meanings of the details, write a one-or two-sentence interpretation.
>God wants me to know that where I go or walk, I have spiritual authority.

How to Hear God's Voice: Intro to Dream Interpretation week four

I N THIS CHAPTER WE WILL introduce three new categories of Dream Language; animals, people, and objects. Whenever an animal, person, or objects are in a dream, there are three questions to ask.

What do the scriptures say about this animal, this person, and/or this object?

What are the natural aspects of this animal, this person, and/or this object?

What does this animal, person, and/or object mean to me?

As you build your dream language with God, He will use the natural tendencies of the object or animal or person. After all, He created this animal, this person, and this object. However, He will also use your feelings toward these things. For example: there is a dog in your dream. You love dogs. You think of a dog as your friend. A dog in your dream might represent friendship. However, what if you are afraid of dogs? You hate dogs. A dog in your dream may represent fear. Again, there are no recipes for dream interpretations. God knows you better than you know yourself. He will talk to you using your reference points, therefore creating your own dream language. So as you remember your dream and certain details stick out, ask yourself these three questions: What does the Bible say about this? What are the natural tendencies of this detail? What are my feelings toward this detail? As we look at examples, this will become clearer.

Dream Language: Animals

Let's begin by using a lion as an example. In the scriptures Jesus is called the Lion of Judah (see Rev. 5:5). On the other hand, Satan is described as a lion who roams around looking for whom he may devour (see 1 Peter 5:8). If you were to have a lion in your dream, you must ask yourself some questions. What do the scriptures say about the animal? Ask God what He is trying to tell you through the lion in your dream.

What if you have a dream about a sheep? What does the Bible say about sheep? They are mute and need a shepherd. Could it mean God is bringing people into your life that need shepherding or mentoring?

Let's say you have a dream about a badger. Where does the Bible refer to a badger? In Exodus where God is giving instructions for the covering for the tabernacle, a badger is mentioned. Is God talking to you about being covered in His presence? What are the natural characteristics of a badger? They are fierce animals. They dig and they bite. Could this dream mean God is warning you of an attack?

What if you have a wolverine in your dream? If you have gone to University of Michigan, a wolverine could mean school pride or team unity. However, if you have not gone to U of M, a wolverine can mean something vicious or destructive.

As you can see, there are many ways to look at the possible meanings of animals. There is no recipe to interpreting a dream. God wants to be a part of this puzzle-solving process. Always ask God what He is trying to say through the use of these animals.

Here is a chart to use as a springboard for the meaning of animals. As a reminder, I have copied this list in the appendix at the end of this study. I have also left space for you to write scriptures you may find with these animals or to add animals that are in your dreams.

Animals

Alligator--big mouth, bossy, will chew you up, hide just before they attack

Bird--varying levels of leadership

Butterfly--transformation

Cat--witchcraft (think of Halloween), watchers

Deer--sincerity (you are a dear) desiring more of God

Dog--(+) friends; (-) enemy

Donkey--(+) peace ;(-) stubborn

Dove--Holy Spirit

Elephant--old memories, unforgiveness

Fish--evangelism

Horse--power

Lion--(+) Power of God/Praise;(-) Satan

Owl--(+) wisdom; (-)occult

Sea turtle--slowness, thoughtfulness, perseverance

Snake--long tale, false accusations

Squirrel--ability to prepare for the future (storing nuts for winter)

Whale--below surface, large hidden movement, deep things of God, big impact

Let's practice interpreting:

Dream: A bear bit my dog, Buddy, on the neck. I grabbed the bear by the neck and the mouth and forced it to let go of Buddy. I shut the door so he couldn't get in the house. I remembered that if a bear snuggled with their heads they go to sleep. I opened the door and pushed my head into his neck and forced him to snuggle to calm him down.

* Circle the important facts: bear, Buddy, shut the door, opened the door, head

Interpretation: In this case the bear was attacking, so I know God is speaking to me about a spiritual attack. I shut the door, but I reopened the door. So God is cautioning me to not reopen the door. Head would represent my thoughts. I think I can handle this attack, or calm it down; however, God is warning me I can't. I remembered in the dream if I snuggle the *head* of a bear it will calm down. Did I snuggle the head? No, I snuggled the *neck*. I missed. God is warning me I cannot calm this attack. So, using the meanings of the details, I can write the interpretation. God is warning me of a spiritual attack. I am shutting it out and then letting it back in. I need to take every thought captive and allow God to take care of the attack.

Also, notice the mouth and neck are referred to. Neck can mean "stubbornness" (stiff-necked). Mouth can mean "your words." So there is a warning to not be stubborn and be careful of my words.

Let's look at another example. This dream was sent to me by a relative. Let's break it down in the procedure I want you to use as you interpret your dream or interpret the dreams of others.

Dream: I am cleaning my house. In the bathroom area, I am currently in the hallway on hands and knees when I see a large spider. I want to kill it. I reach for a magazine, but there is a mouse in the magazine, so I decide to kill the mouse first. I take another heavy magazine and squish the mouse. It dies. I get a baggie to dispose of it. But when I go to lift the magazine to dispose of the mouse, there are two dead mice. I have no idea where the spider is.

Question one: Was there any color? Remember that asking about color helps to determine the source of the dream. I asked the dreamer this question, and she said there was color, but not a specific color that stood out. So we can conclude that the source of the dream is God. (Hint: you will find when interpreting a dream for someone else, you will have to ask questions.)

Question two: Is the dreamer active or observing? Continue practicing; the answers are at the end of Journal Week Four.

What are the important details?
    1.
    2.
    3.
    4.
    5.

What are the meanings of the details?
    1.
    2.
    3.
    4.
    5.

Using the meanings of the details, write a one-to three-sentence interpretation.

Dream Language: People

If you have a dream with people in it, an important question to ask is: Am I observing or am I active in the dream? This was discussed earlier, but it bears repeating. This is the most common mistake people make when interpreting dreams--they forget to ask if they are observing or if they are active. People tend to assume that the dream is about the person in the dream. To avoid this mistake, always ask yourself: Am I observing or am I active?

If I am observing the dream, I am a spectator. If I am taken out of the dream, the dream can still take place. In this case, the dream is about the person in the dream. Most of the time, God is calling you to intercede or pray for the person in the dream. For example, a friend sent me this dream to share.

Example of an Inactive Dreamer:

Dream: I am in a doctor's office; the doctor's daughter comes into the room. She is covered in spots, open sores. I am off to the side and someone is trying to sell me some make-up. I think to myself, I am allergic to make-up. Then a young man comes into the doctor's office. He, too, is covered in these open sores. When I woke up, as I was writing this dream down, my husband told me there was a measles outbreak in town.

First question: Is there any color, or is the dream in black and white? When I asked my friend this, she said it was in color but didn't remember a specific color. Therefore, the source of the dream is God.

Second question: is the dreamer observing or active? In this dream the dreamer is observing most of the dream. There is a side activity where someone is trying to sell the dreamer make-up. However, this is not important to the dream and is a distraction more than an important detail. So, go back to the question: Is the dreamer active or observing? We can determine this by asking if the dreamer is taken out of the dream, does the dream or story still take place? When you take the dreamer out of the dream, the daughter and the young man can still enter the doctor's office.

What are the important details?
1. Doctor's office
2. Young people coming into office with open sores.

What do these details mean?
1. Doctor's office would mean healing
2. Young people with sores would mean there are many.

Interpretation: I believe this dream is God calling the dreamer to pray for healing for the measles outbreak in her town.

This leads to another point. When you wake up from a dream, note how you feel, what you sense, and what you hear. It will be fairly easy, because God wants to talk to you, and He will be faithful to give you all the details you need. In this case, it was no coincidence that the first thing my friend heard was "a measles outbreak."

Another Example of an Inactive Dreamer:

In a dream my friend sent me, she was in a garage with lots of different trucks. There was a woman in the garage that she knew and was supposed to talk to. However, there were photographers there, and they were taking pictures. My friend was moving and trying to stay out of the pictures. The photographers did not notice her and kept taking pictures.

In the dream, my friend is active; however, she is not really part of the story. The photographers continued to take pictures. They didn't notice her. If my friend is taken out of the dream, the action of the story continues. In this dream, the dreamer (my friend) is observing the action and, therefore the dream is about the woman in the dream, not the dreamer.

When determining if the dream is about you, always ask yourself, "If I am taken out of the dream, does the dream still happen?"

If I am active in the dream, the dream is about me. If I remove myself from the dream, does the dream still happen? If the answer is "No, the dream does not happen," then you can conclude the dream is about the dreamer. If the dreamer is the main character in the dream, then the dream is about the dreamer. All the details are about the dreamer, and the person/people in the dream are symbolic. The next question is, "How do I interpret what the meaning is of the person in my dream?"

There are three questions to ask when interpreting the meaning of people.

1. What do the scriptures say about this person?

2. What are the natural aspects of this person?

3. What does this person mean to me?

Let's look at an example of a dream with a father in it.

Dream: I am with my dad. He goes out to the water. It's dark like nighttime. My dad walks out and someone yells to me that there is a fence that will keep me from getting to the water. But my dad keeps going and the fence disappears. My dad walks into the water and keeps going. I see there is a dock. One of its brackets has fallen so I grab it and push it into the dirt so it can stand up again and brace the dock. I walk out onto the dock. Dad is way out there swimming. I try to go out that far; a section of the dock has fallen into the water. I don't care, I go into the water.

Remember the procedure . . .

Is there any color in the dream? As I wrote this down in my dream journal, I did not mention a specific color, but I do recall it was in color. Therefore the source of the dream was God.

Is the dreamer observing or active? I am active so the dream is about me and the people in the dream are symbolic.

Next, what does the scripture say about a father? Jesus used the phrase "Heavenly Father" many times (Matt. 6:14, 26, 32), so this dream is about my relationship with God.

Let's keep going.

What are the important details? (Answers after Journal Week Four)
    1. Dad
    2.
    3.
    4.
    5.

What are the meanings of the details?
    1. Dad--God
    2.
    3.
    4.
    5.
    6.

Using the meanings of the details, write a one-or two-sentence interpretation.

    Let's try a dream with a husband in it.

Dream with a husband in it:
    I thought I was following my husband. I was driving, and I was very tired. I was falling asleep at the wheel. I almost ran into someone because my eyes were closed. I decided to pull over at the next exit. As I looked down, I realized I was going ninety-five miles per hour. I

tried to slow down; as I did, I swerved. There were cars on both side of me; I realized they were police officers. One did a U-turn. I pulled off, and my husband was parked in another area. I wondered if I was following him or if he was following me. My husband came to the car, and I asked if he knew how fast we were driving.

* Ask the dreamer: Was there any color in your dream? I didn't mention any color, but I recall it was in color. What does this tell you, the interpreter? The source of the dream is who? God.

* Is the dreamer active or observing in the dream? The dreamer is active, so the dream is about the dreamer, and the people are symbolic. There are two types of people in this dream: a husband and police officers.

> *"For your Maker is your husband, The Lord of hosts is His name; And your Redeemer is the Holy One of Israel; He is called the God of the whole earth"* (Isa. 54:5).

* What would "husband" represent?

* What would "police officers" represent? This one is a little tricky because there is not a scriptural reference to police. So what are the natural aspects of a police officer? Their job is to uphold the law, to give protection. They have authority.

* Let's keep going. What are the other important details?
  1. Husband
  2.
  3.
  4.
  5.

* What are the meanings of the details?
  1. Husband--God
  2.
  3.
  4.
  5.

Using the meanings of the details, write a one-or two-sentence interpretation. (Remember to check your answers to the answers provided at the end of Journal Week Four.)

Let's do another dream with a person that has a scriptural reference: children. The Bible tells us that children are a gift from God (Ps. 127:3-5). Therefore, whenever a child is in your dream, it has to do with your gifting or talents.

Dream: I was watching my son play soccer. Instead of passing and doing plays, the players were all bunched together. When my son came off the field, he wanted me to carry his stuff. I said no. I thought it was time for him to be independent. I helped him pack his stuff into a suitcase. He carried the suitcase, and I carried his pillow and blanket. I recall the dream was in color.

* Is the dream in color or black or white? Who is the source?

* Is the dreamer active or observing? Who is the dream about?

* What are the important details?
    1. My son
    2.
    3.

* What are the meanings of the details?
    1.My son--gifting (Hint: the dreamer's gifting in this case is teaching and training people.)
    2.
    3.

* Using the meaning of the details, write a one-or two-sentence interpretation.

Let's try an example where there is a person in my dream but it has no scriptural reference.

Dream: I remember the dream was in color. I was supposed to be in a rocket to be launched. Julie Andrews and Shirley Jones and a bunch of men and I were to go up in the rocket. I was driving us in a car. We couldn't find our way there. We were driving along unpaved roads. We stopped at a diner/arcade to get directions. I didn't listen very closely, so we were on back, rough roads again.

* Who is the source of the dream and why?

* Is the dreamer active or observing? What does this tell the interpreter?

* What are the important details?

Notice there are two women that are not in the Bible: Julie Andrews and Shirley Jones. Both these women have great singing careers. I would interpret this to mean "singing" or "praise."

* List the important details.
    1. Julie Andrews and Shirley Jones
    2.
    3.

* What are the meanings of the details?
    1. Julie Andrews and Shirley Jones--singing or praise
    2.
    3.

* Using the meaning of the details, write a one-or two-sentence interpretation.
There are also times when a person in a dream can be interpreted by using the meaning of their name.

Dream: I am running. I am surprised at how easy it is. I notice I am holding myself, and I am not bouncing. I am surprised at how far I can go, and I keep going. My sister-in-law Rebecca is helping me with something. She keeps telling me, "It will be okay. You can do this." The dream seems so bright and cheerful.

* Is there color?

* Who is the dream about?

* What are the important details?
1.
2. Rebecca

* What are the meanings of the details?
1.
2. Rebecca means "refreshed."

* Using the meaning of the details, write a one-or two-sentence interpretation.

Remember, there are no recipes to interpreting dreams; it is a puzzle. Ask God to guide you and for the interpretation. Dreams are about God wanting to talk to you. He will be faithful to explain. For a biblical meaning of names, I use a book *The Name Book: Over 10,000 Names--Their Meanings, Origins, and Spiritual Significance* by Dorothy Astoria.

Dream Language: Objects

A dream will often have an object that sticks out in your memory. Think of the object and what its functions are. For example: If money is present in the dream, the question is: "What is the purpose of money?" When Abraham sent his servant to find a wife for Isaac, he sent many gifts of money and animals. Why? Abraham sent his servant with gifts so that his servant would have favor with the father of the potential wife. He sent the money so that the father would listen to the proposal.

In our society, money means power and influence. When there is money in your dream, ask God what it could mean: favor, power, influence?

Dream with money:

I remember there was color. I was at a window of a bank in a car, someone was in the car with me but I don't know who. I was getting money out. The teller counted out ten-dollar bills, but every other bill was a five-dollar bill. She yelled back to someone that the till was wrong. An older man came behind her with a different stack of money. He counted it correctly and gave it to me.

* First question: Is there color?

* Second question: am I active or observing? The money is being given to me, so I am active.

* What are the important details?
1.
2.
3.

* What are the meanings of the details?
1.
2.
3.

* Using the meaning of the details, write a one-or two-sentence interpretation.

Let's look at some other objects that may appear in a dream. Remember to ask God to guide you and give you a verse where possible.

What could steak mean, or any type of food? It could mean spiritual food, with steak being a more mature kind of food. Paul said he wished that he could give the early Christians meat, but they were still on milk (1 Cor. 3:2 and Heb. 5:12).

What do you think coffee could mean? People often drink coffee in the morning to wake themselves up. In the scriptures God often calls His people to arise and awake. (Judg. 5:12 and Isa. 52:1).

What do you think a cell phone could mean? What does a cell phone do, or how do we use it? We use it for communication. Therefore, a cell phone in a dream may represent communication.

What do you think a type of weaponry might mean, a gun or a knife? What are these used for? What are their purposes? Remember, in a dream things are symbolic. So weaponry usually means some type of spiritual attack. The bigger the weapon, the bigger the spiritual attack. In this instance, the dream is a warning dream. Do not fear; God is protecting you by warning you. Ask Him for strategies to deal with the attack. Your weapons are not carnal, but spiritual (see 2 Cor. 10:4).

Let's look at some possible objects:

Dream: I was shopping at Meijer's Grocery Store. I had purchased two car batteries and forgot to pick them up. I went to the service desk, but they couldn't help me without the receipt. (They could, but it was a real runaround.) So I went to the van in the parking lot and asked my niece if she had seen the receipt. She handed it to me with a big smile. I went back in, and they gave me the batteries and paperwork, saying the next time I needed a battery, I should use the paperwork to call and order. It would be easier.

* Just thinking about the object of a car battery, what do you think the battery could represent?

* Is there a scriptural reference to this object?

* What is this object used for?

* Does it have any personal meaning to the dreamer?

* Using your answers, what do you think a car battery could represent?

Dream: I was in line to get immunization shots. The boy ahead of me was getting the same shots as I was. The nurse was giving them to him in the legs. They were causing him tremendous pain, so much so I had to turn my head and look away. When it was my turn, the nurse put them into my inside arm. She had to put the needle in and pick up the skin and go through to the other side of the skin, pull back a little, and dispense the medicine. When she did it, the shot did not hurt. One shot, two shots, but she messed up on the third shot and had to do it a second time. Afterwards I went to the hospital administrator's office.

* Just thinking about the object of immunization shots, what do you think the shots could represent?

* Is there a scriptural reference to this object; an immunization shot?

* What is this object used for?

* Does this object have any personal meaning to the dreamer?

* Using your answers, what do you think immunization shots could represent?

Let's recap:

Whenever you have an animal, person, or an object in your dream, remember to ask yourself three questions.

1. What do the scriptures say about this animal, this person, and/or this object?

2. What are the natural aspects of this animal, this person, and/or this object?

3. What does this animal, person, and/or object mean to the dreamer?

Remember, dream language is always symbolic and not literal.

Journal Week Four

Make a list of the things you can do to prepare to dream.

1.

2.

3.

4.

5.

6.

7.

Which preparations have you tried?

Which preparations seem to prepare you the best for dreaming?

Which preparations didn't seem to affect your readiness to dream?

Keep trying various ways. Remember, this is about getting you ready to listen to God. It's about focusing on God. It's about getting closer to your Creator, your Father, and your Friend.

Go back to Week Three and write the meaning of the animals, people, and objects you have had in a dream. Add these meanings to the appendix Dream Language.

Again this week, I want you to write down any dreams that you remember. It does not matter if it was just one item or one number. It is important to keep practicing.

Dream 1

Dream 2

Dream 3

Dream 4

Dream 5

This week, do a mindless activity while speaking your dream out loud. For example: try walking and speaking your dream out loud, (washing dishes, taking a shower, raking, etc). Doing a mindless activity can unlock your mind. It can help move your thought process from literal to symbolic. I often do this when I am struggling with understanding a dream.

Which mindless activity did you choose?

Did you receive an interpretation? Write it down. Thank God for it.

Make a list of types of transportation or buildings you had in dreams this week.

1.

2.

3.

4.

5.

(We will discuss the meanings of transportation and buildings in the next chapter. You can write the meaning to these after the lesson)

Remember during the times you are reading scriptures to make note of scriptures that have things that are on your Dream Language list. It will give you a solid reference when further interpreting.

Answers to Interpretation Practice:

Dream with animals in it:

First question: yes, there was color; therefore, the source of the dream is God.

The dreamer is active in the dream; therefore, the dream is about the dreamer.

What are the important details?

1. Bathroom
2. Hallway
3. Hands and knees
4. Mouse
5. Spider

What are the meanings of the details?

1. Deliverance
2. Transition
3. Praying
4. Destructive
5. Occult

Using the meanings of the details, write a one-to three-sentence interpretation.

As you continue to pray, God will bring deliverance to you. You are in a transition, so it seems hard and like you can't get it all, but God will reveal as you seek Him.

Dream with father/dad in it:

Is there color? Yes, therefore God is the source of the dream.

Is the dreamer active? Yes, therefore the dream is about the dreamer.

What are the important details?

1. Dad
2. Water
3. Following Dad, fence disappears
4. Dock broken, I try to fix it
5. Dad goes deeper into water
6. I follow

What are the meanings of the details?

1. Dad--God
2. Water--Holy Spirit

3. Following Dad--following God; fence disappears--boundaries disappear

4. Dock broke, I try to fix it--distraction

5. Dad goes deeper into the water--God wants to take me deeper in the Spirit

6. I follow--that's a good thing

Using the meanings of the details, write a one-or two-sentence interpretation.

God wants to take me into the deeper things of the Spirit. Don't get distracted and try to fix the old things. God will remove the boundaries as I follow Him.

Dream with husband and not scriptural person reference:

Is there color? Yes, therefore the source of the dream is God.

Is the dreamer active? Yes, therefore the dream is about the dreamer.

What are the other important details?

1. Husband

2. Driving tired

3. Going ninety-five miles per hour

4. Police officers on both sides of me

5. I didn't know if my husband was in front of me or behind.

What are the meanings of the details?

1. Husband--God

2. Driving tired--in my own strength

3. Going 95=9+5=14 or double anointing

4. Police on both sides--protection on both sides (Isaiah 30:21)

5. I didn't know if my husband was in front of me or behind me--the Lord goes before us and behind us (Ps. 139:5).

Using the meanings of the details, write a one-or two-sentence interpretation.

God wants me to know He is with me and not to rely on my own strength. He is before me, beside me, and behind me.

Dream with a person that has a scriptural reference (children):

Is there color? Yes, the source of dream is God.

Is the dreamer active? Yes, the dream is about dreamer.

What are the important details?

1. I am watching my son play soccer.

2. When he asks for my help, I tell him no.

3. I still help him carry his stuff.

What are the meanings of the details?
1. my child--my gifting
2. When he asks for help I tell him no--letting him do it himself
3. I still help him carry his stuff--I will still be a part of his life, and help him differently

Using the meaning of the details, write a one-or two-sentence interpretation.

Interpretation: The Bible tells us that children are a gift from God; therefore this dream is about my gifting and talents. My gift is to help people, to train them. There comes a time when I have to let them go and let them become independent. This dream is encouraging me to let people grow in their gifts and that I will still be a part of their lives, just at a different capacity.

Dream with a person that has no scriptural reference:
Is there color? Yes, God is the source of dream.
Is the dreamer active? Yes, therefore the dream is about the dreamer.

What are the important details?
1. Rocket launch
2. Julie Andrews and Shirley Jones
3. I didn't listen very closely.

What are the meanings of the details?
1. Rocket launch--ministry, going high in the things of the Spirit (next week we discuss transportation and how it means a type of ministry)
2. Julie Andrews and Shirley Jones--singing, praise
3. I didn't listen very closely--I need to listen and obey.

Using the meaning of the details, write a one-or two-sentence interpretation.

God wants to tell me that praise will bring me closer to the Lord and higher in the Spirit. (Ps. 150). He is also telling me I need to listen and obey, and when I do, it will keep me on the smoother road.

Dream with a person whose name has a significant meaning:
Is there color? Yes, it was bright and cheery. The source is God.
Is the dreamer active? Yes, the dream is about the dreamer.

What are the important details?
1. I am running with ease.
2. Rebecca is with me and encouraging me.

What are the meanings of the details?
1. I am running with ease--I am doing what I am supposed to do and going where I am supposed to go.
2. Rebecca is with me and encouraging me--her name means refreshed.

Using the meaning of the details, write a one-or two-sentence interpretation.
God wants me to know that I am on the right path and that He is refreshing me along the way.

Dream with money:
Is there color? Yes, the source is God.
Is the dreamer active? Yes, the dream is about the dreamer.

What are the important details?
1. I am getting money .
2. Ten
3. Five

What are the meanings of the details?
1. I am getting money--favor
2. Ten--Journey
3. Five--Grace

Using the meaning of the details, write a one-or two-sentence interpretation.
God is giving me favor (money) and grace (five) for the journey (ten).

How to Hear God's Voice: Intro to Dream Interpretation week five

I N THIS CHAPTER, TRANSPORTATION AND buildings/rooms will be introduced as dream language categories. These categories will require similar questions as the previous categories. Is there a scriptural reference? What are their natural functions? What do they represent to the dreamer?

Dream Language: Transportation

In general, transportation means a type of ministry. In order to spread the gospel, Paul was moved by a ship and by a horse. The transportation is what moved his message that Jesus Christ is the Messiah. When we have a form of transportation in our dreams, we can assume that God is talking to us about a ministry. We have to ask God about the transportation. How big is it? Who is driving? Who or what is powering it?

For example, if you are riding a bike in a dream, it is a small ministry *and* it is powered by you. In addition, a bike can go into tight areas; it can go through rough terrain. So at first you may think it is negative because it is self-propelled. However, you have to ask God questions about it. It may be that God is not correcting you, but encouraging you that He wants you to go into areas that no one else has. It is important to ask God question when interpreting your dreams.

If your dream has a bus and you are not driving, you have to ask what kind of bus it is. Is it a school bus? It may mean a ministry with children or education. If it is a tour bus, it may mean a ministry that will give people fun and adventure. If you are not driving, that would mean God is driving. Let's look at some examples and then make a list to springboard your dream language.

Let's practice:

Dream: I am driving through a construction area, the road is all gravel. I come to a stop sign, and I stop for a very long time. There is no one there to change the sign. No one is coming, so I go forward. In my rearview mirror I see a police car pull out. I pull over. The officer comes up; he is crying. "Do you know how fast you were going?" I thought I was going slowly. He talks and cries about the dangers and how many are getting hurt. I start to feel tears in my eyes. I notice that I am wearing orange nail polish. The policeman tells me to pull ahead, and he will catch up to me. I start to drive slowly and rub the nail polish off. I feel like the policeman has given me mercy and will let me go without a ticket.

* Ask the dreamer if there is any color. (As the dreamer, I remember the orange nail polish.)

* Is the dreamer active or observing?

* What are the important details?

* What are the meanings of the details?

* Using the meanings, write a one-to three-sentence interpretation.

Another example:

Dream: I am on a big cruise ship. A man and his sister have shot the president of Israel. Both are captured and taken off the ship. My husband comes to my side. We go below to an observation deck. We are sitting in one spot, and cannot see, so we move when people leave to sit by a huge window. We see a huge ocean animal. Its teeth are huge and it is hungry. It tries to eat the ship; it cannot, so it leaves. My husband leaves to go upstairs. I scoot my chair back so others can get a chance to see. My husband comes back, and we sit close to the window again.

* Ask the dreamer if there is any color? As the dreamer, I remember it was in color, but nothing specific.

* Is the dreamer active or observing?

* What are the important details?

* What are the meanings of the details?

* Using the meanings, write a one-to three-sentence interpretation.

Let's work on making a list of meanings of transportation. Remember to think about their natural uses as you ask God for their spiritual meanings. Think about size: How many people can it carry? Think about where they go: What kind of terrain? If it goes in the water, it could represent moving in the Spirit. If it goes in the air, it could mean going up with the Lord. All these facets will help in determining what they might mean in a dream.

Airplane: How big is it? Are you driving? What color is it? If you don't remember any of these details, don't worry. It just means the details were not important. An airplane goes up in the sky, so God is talking to you about a ministry that goes up with Him. It also will cover a lot of territory.

Bike: How is it powered? What is the color? What type of bike is it: BMX, Harley Davidson, etc.?

Boat: What type is it? What powers it: wind, motor, paddles?

Car: What color? What kind: race car, sedan, convertible?

Train: How many cars? What type of train? What is it hauling? Coal, food, fuel, animals, etc.

Remember, the bigger the transportation vehicle, the larger the number of people that will be affected by the ministry.

Dream Language: Buildings and Rooms

Recall the parable that Jesus told about the two men who built houses in Matthew 7.

[24] "Therefore whoever hears these sayings of Mine, and does them, I will liken him to a wise man who built his house on the rock: [25] and the rain descended, the floods came, and the winds blew and beat on that house; and it did not fall, for it was founded on the rock.
[26] "But everyone who hears these sayings of Mine, and does not do them, will be like a foolish man who built his house on the sand: [27] and the rain descended, the floods came, and the winds blew and beat on that house; and it fell. And great was its fall."
[28] And so it was, when Jesus had ended these sayings, that the people were astonished at His teaching, [29] for He taught them as one having authority, and not as the scribes.(Matt. 7:24-29)

In this parable, the houses represented the men. So in a dream, buildings and houses represent the dreamer. Keep in mind the purposes of these rooms and what activity is done in these rooms. It will help lead to the interpretation of specific rooms. Don't forget to ask God for scriptural references.

Let's make a list of possible meanings of rooms:

House-self
    Hallway-transition, moving from one room to another
    Bathroom or toilet-a place where one relieves himself or gets rid of waste, deliverance
    Bedroom or bed-a place where one rests or is intimate with one's spouse, intimacy, rest, asleep spiritually
    Kitchen-a place where one prepares food, preparing spiritual food
    Garage-a place of repair
    Basement-a place of hidden things
    Apartment-a place you rent for a length of time, a temporary place
    Hospital-a place of healing
    Hotel-a place you rent for a very short time, a temporary place
    Grocery Store-a place of getting spiritual food
    Warehouse-place of storing goods
    Office-work, calling, occupation
    Church-worship, fellowship, spiritual food, protection (sanctuary)

Let's practice:

Dream: I am in an apartment with my two sons (they are not my sons in real life). They are playing with building toys, but we are supposed to be packing because we are moving.

Oftentimes a specific color will not stick out. However, always ask the question, "Was there any color?" In this case, I do not remember a specific color. I remember that it was in color; therefore God is the source of the dream.

Am I active or observing? It may appear that I am observing in this dream; however, I do not know the boys in my dream. I am the only other character; therefore the dream is about me.

What are the details?
    1. In an apartment
    2. Two sons--two children
    3. Building toys
    4. Supposed to be moving

What are the meanings of the details?
    1. In an apartment--temporary place
    2. Two sons--two children=multiple gifting or talents
    3. Building toys--God is building my gifts or talents
    4. Supposed to be moving--get ready to move or transition

* Using the meanings of the details, write a one-or two-sentence interpretation.

    God is encouraging me that I am growing in my talents/gifting. I am not to get discouraged, because this is a temporary time, and I need to get ready to move forward.

Another example of rooms or buildings:

    Dream: I am walking down many hallways, pushing a walker. I go through the kitchen and more hallways. All the walls are a stained orange. Suddenly the floor gets dirty and muddy, and oily. I feel lost and turned around. The dream was in color.

* Was there color? Yes. Who is the source of the dream? _____

* Am I active or observing? _____ Who is the dream about?

* What are the important details?
    1.
    2.
    3.
    4.
    5.
    6.

* What do the details mean?
    1.
    2.
    3.
    4.
    5.
    6.

* With the meanings of the details, write a on-to three-sentence interpretation.

Another example of rooms and buildings:

Dream: I was lying in bed studying to teach a math class. I had a revelation that certain formulas form the Star of David. I was excited in preparation for teaching the class. Once in the classroom, I was the student teacher, and the head teacher sat in a student's desk to watch. I tried to teach the revelation, but I didn't have it. I felt like I couldn't clearly communicate what I had learned while in my bed. The kids were disruptive. I had to stop and wait for them to be quiet. I was frustrated.

* Is there color? Yes, I remember color in the dream, but nothing specific. Who is the source of the dream?

* Am I observing or active? Who is the dream about?

* What are the important details?

* What are the meanings of the details?

* Using the meanings of the details, write a one-to three-sentence interpretation.

Another example of rooms and buildings:

Dream: I was getting prepared to teach a seminar, getting a poster and chalkboard prepared. I had to go to the bathroom. I walked through the hallway and brought my mom along. I got to the bathroom, and there was a greenish tint to the bathroom. I noticed a snake in the toilet water. I flushed it down. There was a chicken hawk in the other toilet. I flushed it down. I went back to the classroom.

* Is there color? Who is the source of the dream?

* Am I observing or active? Who is the dream about?

* What are the important details?

* What are the meanings of the details?

* Using the meanings of the details, write a one-to three-sentence interpretation.

Let's try a dream with many symbols:

Dream with person, place, number, and transportation:
I am watching my two-year-old nephew. My father drives up in an old '57 blue Dodge car. He opens the garage door, and he brings a wooden box for Graham to put his boots in. He also brings a comforter that I hang by the door. Graham and I and my father hang out in the garage. I look for paper towel because there is vomit in a couple of places on the floor. I am naked, and I slip in some vomit.

* Is there color? Who is the source of the dream?

* Am I active or observing in the dream? Who is the dream about?

* What are the important details to the dream?
    1. Father
    2. Car
    3. Garage
    4. Comforter
    5. Nakedness
    6. 57
    7. Vomit

* What are the meanings of the details?
    1.
    2.
    3.
    4. Holy Spirit
    5. Nakedness in a dream means humility.
    6.
    7. Vomit in a dream means deliverance.

* Using the meanings, write a one-or three-sentence interpretation.

Journal Week Five

We have discussed what to do to prepare to dream. Let's talk about **what to do once you have had a dream.**

1. Write down the dream. This shows God that you are respecting that He is talking to you. Write down the details you remember. It doesn't have to be written in complete sentences or proper grammar. What is important are the details. What colors do you remember? What objects were in the dream? Were there people or animals that you remember in the dream? What feelings did you have when you woke up? What was the main point of the story? What activities were you doing? Do you remember any phrases?

Sometimes dreams are hard to remember. It is helpful if you can turn off your alarm so that the alarm does not jerk you out of the dream. I have a light by my bed with a journal and a pen. No matter the time, when I wake from my dream, I write it down. Otherwise I might forget it. However, God is good. I have forgotten and have asked God to bring it back to me. Remember, He wants to talk to me. So in His faithfulness, sometime during the day I usually remember some detail that helps me know what God wanted to tell me. I quickly write it in my journal!

2. Another thing I try to remember is to double-space when I write the dream down. That way I have room to go back and circle important elements of the dream. If there is a number or color, I have room to write the meaning near the word, which helps me see the interpretation.

3. Next I look for scriptures that have the objects or details that were in my dream. God will always confirm Himself. Whatever He wants to tell you will also be in the Bible. Ask God to guide you to scriptures that confirm what He is saying.

4. Pray! Ask God what He is trying to speak to you about. Ask Him for the interpretation.

5. Start a dream language dictionary. We have discussed many times that there are no recipes for dream interpretation. Write down the unique ways that God is talking to you. What object or color does He often use in your dreams? Start your own chart of colors. Write down the scripture references you have found to confirm that color's meaning. Start a number chart. What numbers has God used to talk to you? Write down the scriptural references. It is important that you have scriptural references to back up your interpretation. That is how many people fall away from a purity or holiness of faith. (Joseph Smith wrote the Book of Mormons from a dream; Muhammad wrote the Koran from a dream.) You have started your dream language as you have added to the appendix.

6. Talk to mature dreamers.

7. Read books on how to biblically interpret dreams. Here is a recommended reading list.
Doug Addison: *Prophecy, Dreams, and Evangelism: Revealing God's Love Through Divine Encounters, Understand Your Dreams Now: Spiritual Dream Interpretation*
Barbie Beathitt: *Dream Encounters, Dreams and Visions of Destiny, Dream See:Searching for the Face of the Invisibler*
Jim Goll: *Dream Language: The Prophetic Power of Dreams, Revelations, and the Spirit of Wisdom , Experiencing Dreams and Visions (Bible study)*
Jane Hamon: *Dreams and Visions: Understanding and Interpreting God's Messages to You*
John Paul Jackson: *The 20 Categories of Dreams, Top 20 Dreams, The Biblical Model of Dream Interpretation*
Perry Stone: *How to Interpret Dreams and Visions: Understanding God's Warnings and Guidance*

***Go back over your journal and pick out one dream you want to interpret. Write it down.

Dream 1:

   * First, find out the source of the dream by asking: Is the dream in color or black and white?

   * Are you active or observing in the dreams? This tells you who the dream is about.

   * Circle the details that may have a meaning in your dream such as colors, numbers, animals, people, buildings, and objects.

   * What are scriptural references to these details?

   * If there are no scriptural references, what does that person or animal mean to you? What are their natural behaviors? What does their name mean?

   * Using the meanings, pray and ask God what He is trying to say to you in this dream. Write out the interpretation He gives you.

Let's talk about **how to handle your dream interpretation.**

1. Write the interpretation down. This shows your respect and thankfulness that God is speaking to you.

2. Don't be upset if you don't get the interpretation right away. It may take some time to understand what God is saying to you. Remember this is a journey. Dreams are meant to grow and enhance your communication with God. Learning takes time. So if you have a blank page for awhile, it is okay. God's timing is perfect. It may be years later and you will think, "*Oh* that's what that dream meant," as you watch the dreams play out before you. Have you ever had a déjà vu moment, like you have been there before? This is an example of recalling a dream.

3. Write a prayer of thankfulness to God for speaking to you.

4. Write a response to God for giving you this dream. Thank Him for instructions or repent if you feel conviction or correction. What are you going to do in response to this dream?

***Go back over your journal and pick out another dream you want to interpret. Write it down.
Dream 2:

    * Is the dream in color or black and white?

    * Are you active or observing in the dreams?

    * Go back and circle details that may have a meaning: colors, numbers, animals, people, buildings, objects.

    * What are scriptural references to these details?

    * If there are no scriptural references, what does that detail mean to you?

    * Using the meanings, pray and ask God what He is trying to say to you in this dream. Write out the interpretation He gives you.

    * Write a prayer of thanksgiving to God for speaking to you.

    * Write what you are going to do about what God has spoken to you about. What is your response to what God is saying?

Write down any dreams you remember.

Dream 1

Dream 2

Dream 3

Dream 4

Dream 5

In Week Three, I gave you different ways to write a dream down (in a circle, on a diagonal). Try this exercise again with a dream you had this week.

* Did you get an interpretation? Write it down.

* Write a prayer of thanksgiving.

* Write your response to God for giving you this dream. What are you going to do in response to this dream?

Answers to Interpretation Practice:

Dream: I am driving through a construction area; the road is all gravel. I come to a stop sign, and I stop for a very long time. There is no one there to change the sign. No one is coming, so I go forward. In my rearview mirror I see a police car pull out. I pull over. The officer comes up; he is crying. "Do you know how fast you are going?" I thought I was going slowly. He talks and cries about the dangers and how many are getting hurt. I start to feel tears in my eyes. I notice that I am wearing orange nail polish on me. The policeman tells me to pull ahead, and he will catch up to me. I start to drive slowly and rub the nail polish off. I feel like the policeman has given me mercy and will let me go without a ticket.

Is there color? There is color: orange nail polish. The dream is from God.
Is the dreamer active or observing? I am active. The dream is about me.

What are the important details?
1. Driving down rough road
2. Police crying because so many are getting hurt
3. Police tells me to continue on and he will catch up to me.
4. I have orange nail polish on my fingers.

What are the meanings of the details?
1. Driving car down rough road--ministry in challenging conditions
2. Authority, showing concern and compassion that so many are getting hurt
3. Encouragement to continue, and He is with me
4. Orange on fingers--perseverance in prayer

Using the meanings, write a one-to three-sentence interpretation.
God has given me a ministry where there are hurting people. He is encouraging me to continue. He is with me; persevere in prayer.

Another example:
Dream: I am on a big cruise ship. A man and his sister have shot the president of Israel. Both are captured and taken off the ship. My husband comes to my side. We go below to an observation deck. We are sitting in one spot, and cannot see, so we move when people leave to sit by a huge window. We see a huge ocean animal. Its teeth are huge and it is hungry. It tries to eat the ship; it cannot, so it leaves. My husband leaves to go upstairs. I scoot my chair back so others can get a chance to see. He comes back, and we sit close to window again.

Ask the dreamer if there is color. I would reply, "Yes, there was color, nothing specific." Therefore, conclude that the source of the dream is God.

Is the dreamer active or observing? The dreamer is active. Therefore, the dream is about the dreamer.

What are the important details?
1. Cruise ship
2. The president is shot.
3. My husband is with me
4. I see a large ocean animal attack the ship.
5. My husband leaves.
6. I move to see better.
7. My husband comes back.

What are the meanings of the details?
1. Ministry with lots of people
2. Danger, but it is taken care of . . . I believe this is God encouraging me that He is taking care of dangerous situations.
3. God is with me.
4. Aware of spiritual attack
5. God moves
6. I move
7. God with me

Using the meanings, write a one-to three-sentence interpretation.

I am part of a ministry that affects a lot of people. There are dangerous situations, but I should not fear because God has it taken care of. God is with me and will show me the dangerous situations. God will move, and I need to stay focused, and I will know that He is with me through it all.

Dream: I am in an apartment with my two sons (they are not my sons in real life). They are playing with colorful building toys, but we are supposed to be packing because we are moving.

Is there color? There is color, so the source is God.

Am I active or observing? It may appear that I am not active in this dream. However, because I do not know the sons that are in my dream, the dream is about me.

What are the details?
1. In an apartment
2. Two sons--two children
3. Building toys
4. Supposed to be moving

What are the meanings of the details?
1. In an apartment--temporary place
2. Two sons--two children--multiple gifting or talents
3. Building toys--God is building my gifts or talents
4. Supposed to be moving--get ready to move or transition

Using the meanings of the details, write a one-or two-sentence interpretation.
God is encouraging me that I am growing in my talents/gifting. I am not to get discouraged, because this is a temporary time, and I need to get ready to move forward.

Dream: I am walking down many hallways, pushing a walker. I go through the kitchen and more hallways. All the walls are a stained orange. Suddenly the floor gets dirty and muddy and oily. I feel lost and turn around.
Is there color? There is color, so the source is God.

Is the dreamer active or observing? I am active, so the dream is about me.

What are the important details?
1. Walking
2. Hallways
3. Kitchen
4. Orange
5. Floor dirty, muddy, oily
6. Feel lost and turn around

What do the details mean?
1. Where I am walking
2. Transition
3. Getting spiritual food
4. Perseverance
5. Difficult walkway
6. Feeling like giving up

With the meanings of the details, write a one-to three-sentence interpretation.

God wants me to know that I am in a transition, and that is why it feels so difficult to walk or move forward. God is teaching or feeding me spiritual things. I need to persevere and not give up.

Dream: I was lying in bed studying to teach a math class. I had a revelation that certain formulas form the Star of David. I was excited to teach the class. Once in the classroom, I was the student teacher, and the head teacher sat in a student's desk to watch. I tried to teach the revelation, but I didn't have it solid, and I felt like I couldn't clearly communicate what I had learned while in my bed. The kids were disruptive. I had to stop and wait for them to be quiet. I was frustrated. I remember color.

Is the dream in color or black and white? The dream is in color; therefore the dream is from God.

Am I observing or active? I am active, therefore the dream is about me.

What are the important details?
1. In bed
2. Had revelation
3. Wanted to teach it
4. Head teacher there to observe
5. I didn't completely understand revelation
6. Kids disruptive
7. Had to wait
8. Frustrated

What are the meanings of the details?
1. In bed--intimacy with God
2. Had revelation--God is speaking to me.
3. Wanted to teach it--I want to teach what God is speaking to me about,
4. Head teacher there to observe--God is watching me.
5. I didn't completely understand revelation--I don't understand fully what God is speaking to me about,
6. Kids disruptive--people not willing to listen
7. Had to wait--God is asking me to wait,
8. Frustrated--be careful not to get frustrated or have bad attitude

Using the meanings of the details, write a one-to three-sentence interpretation.

God is speaking to me about things. God is asking me to spend more time with Him to understand fully and to wait to share with people. I am not to get frustrated, but trust God's timing.

Another example of rooms and buildings:

Dream: I was getting prepared to teach a seminar, getting a poster and chalkboard prepared. I had to go to the bathroom. I walked through the hallway and brought my mom along. I got to the bathroom and noticed there was a greenish tint to everything. I noticed a snake in the toilet water. I flushed it down. There was a chicken hawk in the other toilet. I flushed it down. I went back to the classroom.

Is this dream in color or black and white? There is color in this dream. God is the source of the dream.

Am I observing or active? Active; the dream is about me.

What are the important details?
1. Getting prepared
2. Go to bathroom
3. In hallway
4. Greenish tint to bathroom
5. Snake
6. Chicken hawk

What are the meanings of the details?
1. Getting prepared--God is getting me ready for teaching
2. Go to bathroom--deliverance
3. In Hallway--transition
4. Greenish tint to bathroom--growing, conscience of Holy Spirit leading
5. Snake--lies
6. Chicken Hawk--I don't know much about chicken hawks. Whenever this happens, I go to "Google" and look up information about the subject. In this case, Google led me to Wikipedia where I could read about the traits of chicken hawks. Interestingly, a chicken hawk is a name given to a person that supports war, yet does whatever it takes to avoid being drafted into the war. What stood out to me was: Hypocrisy. In this case, I believe God is using a chicken hawk to represent hypocrisy.

Using the meanings of the details, write a one-to three-sentence interpretation.

God is preparing me to teach and wants to bring deliverance to me. I am in a transition where I am growing in my relationship with the Holy Spirit. With that transition will come deliverance from lying and hypocrisy.

Dream with person, place, number, and transportation:

I am watching my two-year-old nephew. My father drives up in an old '57 blue Dodge car. He opens the garage door, and he brings a wooden box for Graham to put his boots in. He also brings a comforter that I hang by the door. Graham and I and my father hang out in the garage. I look for paper towel because there is vomit in a couple of places on the floor. I am naked, and I slip in some vomit.

Is there color? Yes, the car was blue, therefore the dream is from God.

Am I active or observing in the dream? I am active; therefore the dream is about me.

What are the important details to the dream?
1. Father
2. Blue car
3. Garage
4. Nakedness
5. 57
6. Vomit

What are the meanings of the details?
1. Father--God
2. Blue Car--ministry of revelation
3. Garage--place of repair
4. Nakedness in a dream means humility.
5. Five--grace; seven--complete
6. Vomit in a dream means deliverance.

Using the meanings, write a one-or three-sentence interpretation.

As I stay humble before the Lord, He is preparing me for a ministry of revelation that will be full of grace. That preparation will include deliverance and repairing my heart.

Dream: I am driving through a construction area; the road is all gravel. I come to a stop sign, and I stop for a very long time. There is no one there to change the sign. No one is coming, so I go forward. In my rearview mirror, I see a police car pull out. I pull over. The officer comes up; he is crying. "Do you know how fast you were going?" I thought I was going slowly. He talks and cries about the dangers and how many are getting hurt. I start to feel tears in my eyes. I notice that I am weraring orange nail polish. The policeman tells me to pull ahead, and he will catch up to me. I start to drive slowly and rub the nail polish off. I feel like the policeman has given me mercy and will let me go without a ticket.

Ask the dreamer if there is any color. Yes, there is color. You can conclude that the dream is from God.

Is the dreamer active or observing? The dreamer is active; therefore you can conclude the dream is about the dreamer.

What are the important details?
    1. Driving through a construction area
    2. Officer
    3. Talks of dangers
    4. Orange on fingers
    5. Mercy

What are the meanings of the details?
    1. Driving through a construction area--ministry where things are being worked on
    2. Officer--authority
    3. Talks of danger--God revealing what is going on
    4. Orange--perseverance; Fingers--pray
    5. Mercy--mercy

Using the meanings, write a one-to three-sentence interpretation.
    God is revealing what He is working on. He is giving me authority to work with Him in prayer. I need to have perseverance and pray with mercy as my motive.

Another example:
Dream: I am on a big cruise ship. A man and his sister have shot the president of Israel. Both are captured and taken off the ship. My husband comes to my side. We go below to an observation deck. We are sitting in one spot and cannot see, so we move when people leave to sit by a huge window. We see a huge ocean animal. Its teeth are huge, and it is hungry. It tries to eat the ship; it cannot, so it leaves. My husband leaves to go upstairs. I scoot my chair back so others can get a chance to see. My husband comes back, and we sit close to window again.

Ask the dreamer if there is any color. As the dreamer, I remember it was in color, but nothing specific. Therefore, the source of the dream is God

Is the dreamer active or observing? Active; therefore the dream is about the dreamer.

What are the important details?
1. Big Cruise Ship
2. President of Israel shot
3. Criminals captured
4. Husband with me
5. Go to observation deck
6. We move to see better
7. Huge ocean animal tries to attack ship
8. Husband leaves and comes back

What are the meanings of the details?
1. Big Cruise Ship--ministry that affects a lot of people
2. President of Israel shot--danger
3. Criminals caught--danger will be stopped
4. Husband with me--God with me
5. Go to observation deck--God will show me things
6. We move to see better--move with God to continue seeing things
7. Huge Ocean animal tries to attack ship--spiritual attack on ministry
8. Husband leaves and comes back--It may feel at times that God is not with me, but He always is.

Using the meanings, write a one-to three-sentence interpretation.
God has given me a huge, fun ministry. As I move with Him, He will show me where there is danger. Not to fear, for God has it.

HOW TO HEAR GOD'S VOICE: INTRO TO DREAM INTERPRETATION WEEK SIX

So you have had a dream. Now what?

You have written it down.

You have sought God for an interpretation.

You have written down the interpretation.

How do I know if it's right? Asking yourself these three questions will give you discernment.

1. Does it line up with the word of God?
2. Does it witness to your spirit?
3. Does it encourage, comfort, edify?

These are questions to ask yourself after you have interpreted your dream. Is the interpretation saying the same thing the Bible tells you? Does the interpretation feel right? Is it confirming things that God has been speaking to your spirit already? Does the interpretation encourage you or comfort you in any way? You will feel a peace in your heart or excitement in your spirit. You will feel love and encouragement. Sometimes you will feel as though you are being corrected, but even this will be in a loving and encouraging way.

You feel the interpretation is right; now what?
1. Write a prayer of thanksgiving to God.
For example, one of the first dreams I shared with you was about my daughter handing money to me. The interpretation was that God wanted me to know that He is fulfilling His promises to me concerning my gifts and callings and my debt. A response to this might be,

"Thank You, Lord, for the gift of teaching you have given me. Thank You for fulfilling Your promises to me concerning this gifting."

2. Write a response to the dream. What am I going to do about the dream?

After this dream, I might say to God, "I will trust You, Lord, with my financial situation. I will stop worrying and ask for Your guidance concerning my finances. I will not lean on my own understanding but trust in You with all my heart."

To know how to respond to your dream, it will help you to know what kind of dream you just had.

There are many types of dreams. However, these are the ones I experience most frequently.

Encouragement Dreams:

God loves you. He wants to speak to you to encourage you. Remember how Joseph's dream encouraged him? He was so excited that God wanted to use him as a leader. How wonderful it would be if we all had a dream at a young age that told us God's plans for us. It is never too late! God could give you a dream tonight of his plans of hope and prosperity and love (Jer. 29:11).

Intercession Dreams:

Ninety-nine percent of all dreams are about you. God is talking to you about you. However, there is one instance when God wants to talk to you about others. Now realize, God is *not* into gossip. However, He is very much about lifting each other up in prayer. An intercession dream is for you to pray about the person you are dreaming about. How do you tell if it is about you or about another person? If you are active in a dream, the dream is about you. In other words, if you were taken out of the dream, the dream would not happen. So you are the one who opens the door, or you are the one that the dog comes to, or you are the one swimming in the dream, the dream is about you. If you are observing the dream, the dream is about the main character of the dream. Ask yourself, if I was not here, could the dream still happen? Do I play an active role in this dream? If you have determined that you are only observing and not participating, then the dream is *not* about you. Next you have to ask, "Who is the main character?" "What is the dream revealing to me about this person?" "How do I pray for this person?" I find these kinds of dreams an honor. God trusts me to pray for someone. This is not for me to judge the person. This is not some dark secret into someone's private life. This is God trusting me to pray and intercede for a person that God loves. He wants to move in their life. That is an honor and a privilege. Please regard it as such.

Directional/Warning Dream:

God is a good God. He wants to direct you in the way that you should go. (see Isa. 58:11 and Prov. 3:6) He gave Joseph, Mary's husband, many dreams to guide him from danger. God wants to do the same for you. Dreams will give you directions, and they can give you warnings.

Once you determine what type of dream you have just had, you can respond. Often your response will be something like: "Thank You for Your guidance. I will trust and obey by_____" or "Thank You for sharing this about _____. How do You want me to pray for _____?"

CONCLUSION:

In conclusion, there is no recipe for interpreting dreams. It is an exciting journey of discovering God's love and encouragement, even His corrections. He wants to draw you closer to Him through giving you a dream, a puzzle to work out together. He loves it when you seek Him and promises that you will find Him (see Jer. 33:3).

There is not a recipe; however, there is a process to interpreting a dream. First ask yourself, the dreamer, if there was any color to determine the source. Second, determine if the dreamer is active or observing to discern who the dream is about. Thirdly, ask God to help you recall the important (not all) details and what the meanings of those details are. What scripture references the detail? What are the natural tendencies of the details? What does the detail mean to you? Ask God to put the meanings into a one-to three-sentence interpretation.

To further the value of the dream, honor the Lord by thanking Him for the dream. Respond to the Lord. Tell Him how this dream has moved you and what actions you will take because of the dream. Observe the deepening of your relationship with God as you do this.

Thank you so much for joining me on this adventure.

God bless and sweet dreams.

Journal Week Six

Write down the dreams you have.

Write down the interpretation using the process taught in this study. Who is the source of the dream? Who is the dream about? What are the details? What do the details mean? Write a one-to three-sentence interpretation.

Write a prayer of thanksgiving for the dream.

Write a response to the interpretation.

Dream 1

Dream 2

Dream 3

Dream 4

Dream 5

If you struggle with interpreting a dream, try writing it differently as discussed in Week Three or do a mindless activity as discussed in Week Four. Have fun as you develop your dream language with God. Keep trying and remember God is calling you into a closer relationship with Him.

APPENDIX: DREAM LANGUAGE

I have left space for you, the dreamer, to add to your personal dream language appendix.

Dream Language: Color

White (+) Spirit of the Lord, holy power; (-) religious spirit

Red (+) wisdom, anointing, power; (-) anger, war

Green (+) conscience, growth, prosperity; (-) envy, jealousy, pride

Blue (+) communion, revelation; (-) depression, sorrow, anxiety

Yellow (+) mind, hope, gift of God; (-) fear, coward, intellectual pride

Orange (+) perseverance; (-) stubbornness, strong-minded

Purple (+) authority, royalty; (-) false authority, licentiousness

Dream Language: Numbers

One--God.
Two--witness
Three--God.
Four--creative works.
Five--grace.
Six--man, double
Seven--completion.
Eight--new beginnings.
Nine--fullness
Ten--journey, trials, and testing
Eleven--transition
Twelve--government
Thirteen--rebellion
Fourteen--double anointing
Fifteen--mercy, reprieve
Sixteen--established new beginnings
Seventeen--elect of God
Thirty--begin ministry
Forty--testing
Fifty--jubilee, debt cancelation
One hundred--Child of Promise, fruitfulness, promise fulfilled

Dream Language: Animals

Alligator--big mouth, bossy, will chew you up, hide just before they attack

Birds--varying levels of leadership

Butterfly--transformation

Cat--witchcraft, watchers

Deer--sincerity (you are a dear), desiring more of God

Dogs--(+)friends;(-) enemy

Donkey--(+)peace;(-)stubborn

Dove--Holy Spirit

Elephants--old memories, unforgiveness

Fish--evangelism

Horse--power

Lion--(+)power of God/praise, (-)Satan

Owl--(+)wisdom; (-)occult

Sea turtle--slowness, thoughtfulness, perseverance

Snake--long tail, false accusations

Squirrel--ability to prepare for the future (storing nuts for winter)

Whale--below surface, large hidden movement, deep things of God, big impact

Dream Language: People

Father--God
Husband--God
Wife--the church
Child--gifting or callings

Dream Language: Objects

Money--favor, power, influence
Food--spiritual food
Coffee--wake up, drug (caffeine)
Cell Phone--communication
Weapons--spiritual attack
Car battery--power, recharge, strength
Immunization shot--protection

Dream Language: Transportation

Airplane--spiritual place

Airplane crashing--something is crashing

Airplane on ground--something is keeping you from taking off

Army helicopter--personal ministry with strategic nature

Bike--individual calling, ministry, or job

 Motorcycle--same as bike but more powerful

Boat--Cruise ship: ministry with lots of people having fun

 Speed boat--exciting ministry but shortlived

 Submarine--below the surface, deep in spirit but not seen by many people; maybe you see what others don't see, or God's calling you deeper.

 Tugboat: ministry of helps

Car--personal ministry

 Convertible--open revelation

 Limo--more people

 Getting into car--leaving for ministry

 Pickup truck--small ministry that carries things

 Semitrailer--large ministry that carries provision, blessings, marketplace

 Van--similar to car, more people

 Wrecker--ministry of helping other ministries

Train--movement of God, something God is doing such as a revival

Dream Language: Building/Rooms

House--self

Hallway--transition

Bathroom or toilet--deliverance

Bedroom or bed--intimacy, asleep spiritually

Kitchen--preparing spiritual food

Garage--a place of repair

Basement--a place of hidden things

Hospital--a place of healing

Grocery Store--a place of getting spiritual food

Warehouse--place of storing goods

Office--work, calling, occupation

Church--worship, fellowship, spiritual food, protection

www.ingramcontent.com/pod-product-compliance
Lightning Source LLC
Chambersburg PA
CBHW062112090426
42741CB00016B/3402